Kathleen's
Bake Shop
COOKBOOK

Kathleen's
Bake Shop
COOKBOOK

Kathleen King

Illustrations by Richard Harrington

St. Martin's Press
New York

To Mom and Dad

for teaching me to believe in myself; it is through your wisdom
and inspiration that I have realized that no dream is out of reach.

Design by Judith Dannecker

Library of Congress Cataloging-in-Publication Data

King, Kathleen.
   [Bake Shop Cookbook]
   Kathleen's Bake Shop cookbook / Kathleen King.
      p.   cm.
   ISBN 0-312-03853-4
   1. Baking. 2. Kathleen's Bake Shop. I. Title.
TX765.K525   1990
641.8'65—dc20

                                  89-27043
                                       CIP

First Edition
10 9 8 7 6 5 4

Contents

Acknowledgments

Many thanks to my husband, Mark Cirillo, for his endless patience and support in all that I do.

To Carla Glasser, for convincing me to take on this project.

To my sister-in-law, Robin King, for introducing pies to the bake shop, and for her hard work in the beginning stages.

To Bob Sielaff, for always being there for advice and knowledge.

To the staff at Kathleen's Bake Shop:

Nancy Boden for her years of dedication and support.

Anthony Takacs for his knowledge of the industry.

Michael Cause for his total efficiency day in and day out.

Michelle Strazzere for her cheerful disposition and quality baking.

Cindy Berglin for her willingness to learn and help out.

Harriet Austin for keeping us all young.

Patti Bruzdoski for her smiling face year after year.

Kenny Patrick and Ken Pruess for keeping the baked goods flowing, without fail, to New York City and beyond.

And to Duke for sampling all our baked goods throughout the testing.

Finally, and most importantly, a heartfelt THANK YOU to my loyal customers who have continually supported my efforts since I was eleven years old.

Foreword

Along North Sea Road in the posh summer resort community of South-ampton, New York, one finds a mecca for lovers of old-fashioned, down-to-earth baked goods. Kathleen's Bake Shop has gained a reputation among local farmers and fishermen as well as among the affluent summer residents as the ultimate source for extraordinary bakery products, ranging from sin-fully rich brownies and carrot cakes to delicate scones and fruit pies. It is, undisputably, the quintessential country bakery. The heart and soul of this thriving country kitchen is thirty-year-old Kathleen King-Cirillo. It is from her renowned Southampton bake shop that the recipes in this volume were compiled, created, and tested.

Kathleen's Bake Shop is a bit of a paradox. Its setting, location, and ambience evoke an image of a classic country bakery. The air is filled with the tantalizing aromas of cookies, brownies, pies, and muffins fresh from the oven. Products are displayed on large, country pine tables. Jams, jellies, scones, and croissants rest on an antique hutch where pies might have been placed to cool one hundred years earlier. And visitors are treated to a bird's-eye view of the creative process as workers roll pie crusts and mix ingredients directly behind the counter. At the same time, Kathleen's Bake Shop has developed a loyal following of customers from New York City and environs, lured initially by Kathleen's famous oversized chocolate-chip cookies, and continually attracted by the homespun character of the bake shop and the youthful charm of its creator.

Born in Southampton, Kathleen King spent her childhood in the bucolic setting of North Sea Farms, run by her father, Richard, known locally as "Tate," and her mother, Millie. The youngest of four children, Kathleen divided her time between school and helping out on the dairy and poultry farm. When Kathleen and her siblings weren't candling and sorting eggs they were busy tending to the chickens and cows and ensuring that the family farm was running smoothly. That included seeing to it that the farm stand was well stocked with eggs, poultry, produce, and dairy products.

It was Kathleen's older sister, Karin, who began baking cookies and breads and selling them alongside the other products at the farm stand. Karin, four years older than Kathleen, eventually longed for "a real job" and passed the mixing spoon to Kathleen. Ever the entrepreneur, Kathleen was eager "to earn extra money for school clothes" and assumed the responsibilities of baking for the farm stand. She combined hard work with fresh ingredients to create a recipe for a successful enterprise.

Throughout high school, Kathleen continued to pitch in around the farm, but summers became increasingly devoted to baking. She honed her skills and collected and perfected recipes, and soon the fledgling baking business began to reap real rewards. Kathleen was able to save enough money for tuition at the State University of New York at Cobleskill, where she earned a degree in restaurant management in 1979. After graduation she returned to her roots in Southampton and soon thereafter took the bold step of setting up shop in a rented space in the Village of Southampton. In the spring of 1980 Kathleen's Cookie was born!

It didn't take long for the tenacious Kathleen to carve a comfortable niche in the local marketplace. Many of her year-round and summer customers followed her to the new establishment where they found an expanded array of baked goods. Word spread of her special talents for baking, and soon local, regional, and national publications began recounting the story of Kathleen's enormous popularity. Despite hiring a staff of full-time and part-time assistants, Kathleen logged twenty-hour workdays, six days a week, to keep up with the demand for her products. She tapped the good graces and talents of her sister-in-law, Robin, to help with the pies and with the daily hustle and bustle of a growing business. The business snowballed, and it wasn't long before Kathleen's Cookie outgrew the rented space. By the close of 1983 Kathleen's search for a new storefront and bakery ended. She secured a Victorian house that had once been an Italian restaurant, renovated it, and outfitted the kitchen with enormous revolving steel ovens, refrigeration systems, and mixing apparatus. By the start of the tourist season in 1984, Kathleen's Bake Shop was in business.

Today, Kathleen employs up to thirty people during the peak summer season, and on a busy day the bake shop will make upwards of 7,000 chocolate-chip cookies. Her clientele is vast and varied with loyal customers traveling many miles for a taste of Kathleen's culinary creations. To satiate her New York City customers year-round, Kathleen's Bake Shop opened in Manhattan in the autumn of 1986.

It was an article in *Family Circle* magazine about Kathleen King, her country roots, and her burgeoning bakery business that caught the eye of one Mark Cirillo in Florida. Struck by the similarity of her life-style and philosophy to his own, Mark wrote a letter to Kathleen. The two corresponded, and in 1987 they met for the first time. Friendship evolved into love, and in the spring of 1988 Mark and Kathleen were married in a country wedding in Southampton, with the reception held appropriately at Kathleen's family farm in North Sea.

Kathleen and Mark plan to sail around the world, embarking in 1992, in a fifty-three-foot schooner he is currently building. But Kathleen will not leave her bake shop behind; she will bake cookies in the ship's galley and sell them at ports as their journey progresses.

The recipes in Kathleen's first book (we can only hope there will be more to come) are her way of sharing her gifts with those who have been loyal, faithful customers at the farm, at Kathleen's Cookie, and today at Kathleen's Bake Shop. To those of us who have enjoyed Kathleen's creations over the years, we are grateful that she has elected to share these recipes with us. But it is presumptuous of anyone to believe that he or she will achieve the same results as Kathleen. Her unique country style, her delightful demeanor, and her wonderful disposition are essential ingredients in every product at Kathleen's Bake Shop. They would be difficult to duplicate at home. But thanks, Kathleen, for letting us try.

—HAROLD CLARK
Southampton, New York
June 1989

Cookies

Brownies

This recipe was developed by accident. I always seem to be in a hurry when I bake and read only half the directions. The original recipe called for melting half the chocolate chips and adding half at the end. Well, I melted the whole amount before realizing this. The results were the best brownies I had ever eaten! Do not overbake, or they will be a completely different brownie. They should be a little damp when you remove them from the oven because they will continue to bake in their own heat.

¾ cup all-purpose flour
¼ teaspoon baking soda
¼ teaspoon salt
2 cups semisweet chocolate chips
1 teaspoon vanilla extract

⅓ cup butter
⅔ cup granulated sugar
2 tablespoons water
2 eggs
½ cup chopped walnuts (optional)

1 Preheat oven to 325° F. Grease a 9-inch square pan.

2 In a small bowl, stir together flour, baking soda, and salt.

3 In a large bowl, combine chocolate chips and vanilla.

4 In a saucepan, combine butter, sugar, and water. Bring this mixture just to a boil. Pour hot mixture over chips and stir. Add eggs one at a time, mixing well after each addition. Stir in the flour mixture. Fold in nuts if desired. Pour into prepared pan. Spread evenly.

5 Bake for 30 to 35 minutes, or until slightly firm to touch. When cool, cut into squares. (Brownies freeze well and can be mailed to friends and children at camp.)

Yield: 16 small
brownies

Peanut Butter Squares

Similar in taste to Reese's Peanut Butter Cups, these are easy to make and will save you a trip to the store. Bob Sielaff, a good friend and former teacher, gave me this recipe while I attended the State University of New York at Cobleskill.

¾ cup firmly packed dark-brown sugar
1 pound (3 cups) confectioners' sugar
½ cup butter, softened

2 cups smooth peanut butter
2 cups semisweet chocolate chips
1 tablespoon butter

1 In a large bowl, and using an electric mixer, beat first four ingredients together until smooth and well blended. Pat into ungreased 15½- by 10½- by 1-inch pan. Roll flat on top with rolling pin.

2 Melt chocolate chips and 1 tablespoon butter in the top of a double boiler. Spread over peanut butter mixture and cut into squares while chocolate is still warm and soft.

3 Chill for about 15 minutes and remove from pan. These can last in the refrigerator for weeks.

Yield: forty 2-inch
squares

Chocolate–Peanut Butter Cookies

 Try these if you prefer a cakey, not-too-sweet cookie.

3 squares (3 ounces) unsweetened chocolate
1 cup all-purpose flour
1 teaspoon baking powder
1 teaspoon baking soda
¼ teaspoon salt
¾ cup butter

½ cup granulated sugar
½ cup firmly packed dark-brown sugar
½ cup smooth peanut butter
2 eggs
½ cup semisweet chocolate chips
½ cup chopped peanuts

1 Melt chocolate in the top of a double boiler.

2 In a medium-sized bowl, stir together flour, baking powder, baking soda, and salt.

3 In a large bowl, cream butter, sugars, and peanut butter. Mix in melted chocolate. Beat in eggs. Stir in flour mixture. Fold in chocolate chips and peanuts.

4 Roll dough into a 4-inch-diameter log. Dough will be sticky. Wrap in plastic wrap and refrigerate overnight.

5 When ready to bake, preheat oven to 350° F. Prepare greased cookie sheets.

6 Cut dough in ¼-inch slices and quarter each piece. Place on cookie sheets 1 inch apart and bake for 10 to 12 minutes. Cookies will spread and feel like cake to the touch. Remove cookies to a wire rack to cool.

Yield: 4 dozen cookies

Chocolate-Chip
Oatmeal Cookies

These cookies are a nice change from the traditional chocolate-chip cookie.

1 cup plus 2 tablespoons all-purpose flour
1 cup quick-cooking rolled oats
2 tablespoons Dröste or other cocoa powder
¾ teaspoon baking soda
½ teaspoon salt

¾ cup butter, softened
½ cup firmly packed dark-brown sugar
½ cup granulated sugar
1 teaspoon vanilla extract
1 egg
1 cup semisweet chocolate chips
½ cup chopped walnuts

1 Preheat oven to 350° F. Grease cookie sheets.

2 In a large bowl, stir together flour, oats, cocoa powder, baking soda, and salt.

3 In another large bowl, cream butter, sugars, and vanilla until well blended. Beat in egg. Stir in flour mixture until well combined. Fold in chocolate chips and walnuts. Drop batter by teaspoonfuls onto prepared cookie sheets, leaving 2 inches between cookies.

4 Bake for 10 to 12 minutes, or until slightly firm to touch. Remove cookie sheets and let cookies stand for 2 to 3 minutes before removing them to a wire rack.

Yield: about 5 dozen cookies

Blondies

These are dense, fudgy, bar cookies studded with chocolate chips and walnuts—a great alternative for those who love brownies, but not all the chocolate.

2¼ cups all-purpose flour
1 teaspoon baking powder
¼ teaspoon salt
1 cup butter
1¾ cups firmly packed light-brown
   sugar

2 eggs
2 teaspoons vanilla extract
1 cup chopped walnuts
1 cup semisweet chocolate chips

1 Preheat oven to 350° F. Grease a 13- by 9-inch baking pan.

2 In a large bowl, stir together flour, baking powder, and salt.

3 In another large bowl, cream butter and sugar until light and fluffy. Beat in eggs, one at a time, until well blended. Mix in vanilla. Stir in flour mixture until well blended. Fold in walnuts and chocolate chips. Spread batter evenly in prepared pan.

4 Bake for 35 minutes, or until top springs back when lightly tapped with fingers. Remove pan to a wire rack and let cool before cutting. (Blondies freeze well and can be mailed easily.)

Yield: 24 blondies

Mrs. Patrick's Crinkles

Mrs. Patrick is the mother of our manager and driver. Over the years, we have traded baked goods, and this is one of our favorites. It's very rich and tastes similar to a brownie.

4 squares (4 ounces) unsweetened chocolate, melted
½ cup vegetable oil
2 cups granulated sugar
4 eggs
2 teaspoons vanilla extract

2 cups all-purpose flour
½ teaspoon salt
2 teaspoons baking powder
1 cup semisweet chocolate chips (optional)
1 cup confectioners' sugar

1 Melt chocolate in the top of a double boiler.

2 In a large bowl, mix together oil and sugar. Stir in melted chocolate. Beat in eggs one at a time, mixing well after each addition. Stir in vanilla. Stir in flour, salt, and baking powder. Fold in chocolate chips.

3 Wrap dough in plastic wrap and refrigerate overnight or for at least 2 hours.

4 Preheat oven to 350° F. Prepare greased cookie sheets.

5 Roll dough into walnut-sized balls and then roll balls in confectioners' sugar. Place balls 1 inch apart on cookie sheets and bake for 10 minutes, or until cookies have white cracks on top showing chocolate beneath. Cookies will crack on top. Remove cookies to a wire rack to cool.

Yield: 7 dozen cookies

Peanut Butter
Swirl Bars

 These delicious bars are like peanut butter brownies covered in chocolate.

1 cup all-purpose flour
1 teaspoon baking powder
¼ teaspoon salt
½ cup smooth peanut butter
⅓ cup butter, softened

¾ cup firmly packed dark-brown
  sugar
¾ cup granulated sugar
2 eggs
2 teaspoons vanilla extract
2 cups semisweet chocolate chips

---

1 Preheat oven to 350° F.

2 In a medium-sized bowl, stir together flour, baking powder, and salt.

3 In a large bowl, beat peanut butter, butter, brown sugar, and granulated sugar until creamy. Gradually beat in eggs and vanilla. Add flour mixture.

4 Pour into a greased 13- by 9-inch pan. Sprinkle chips on top of batter. Bake for 3 minutes.

5 Remove from oven and run a knife through at 2-inch intervals to marbleize. Bake for 30 minutes more, until they spring back to touch and an inserted toothpick comes out clean.

Yield: 4 dozen bars

Peanut Butter Cookies

My mother-in-law used to make these for my husband when he was growing up. They're packed with peanut butter flavor and will become an old-time favorite for all peanut butter lovers! Serve with chocolate ice cream or cold milk.

1½ cups all-purpose flour
¼ teaspoon salt
1 teaspoon baking soda
½ cup butter, softened
½ cup firmly packed dark-brown
   sugar

½ cup granulated sugar
1 egg
½ teaspoon vanilla extract
1 cup smooth peanut butter

1 Preheat oven to 375° F. Prepare greased cookie sheets.

2 In a medium-sized bowl, stir together flour, salt, and baking soda.

3 In a large bowl, cream butter and sugars. Add egg and vanilla; mix until well blended. Add peanut butter and mix well. Stir in flour mixture.

4 Roll dough into balls the size of walnuts. Place on prepared cookie sheets and press with a fork in a crisscross pattern.

5 Bake for 10 minutes. Remove cookies to a wire rack to cool.

Yield: 4 dozen 2½-inch
cookies

Chocolate-Chip
Cookies

I have been baking and selling these cookies since I was eleven years old. I haven't changed the recipe all this time, and they remain everyone's favorite. They are thin and slightly crisp cookies. I sell thousands of these a day in my busy season.

2 cups all-purpose flour
1 teaspoon baking soda
1 teaspoon salt
1 cup butter
¾ cup granulated sugar

¾ cup firmly packed dark-brown
   sugar
1 teaspoon water
1 teaspoon vanilla extract
2 eggs
2 cups semisweet chocolate chips

1 Preheat oven to 350° F. Prepare greased cookie sheets.

2 In a large bowl, stir together flour, baking soda, and salt.

3 In another large bowl, cream butter and sugars. Add water and vanilla. Mix until just combined. Add eggs and mix lightly. Stir in the flour mixture. Fold in chocolate chips. Don't overmix.

4 Drop onto prepared cookie sheets using two tablespoons. Cookies will spread, so space them at least 2 inches apart.

5 Bake for 12 minutes, or until edges and center are brown. Remove cookies to a wire rack to cool.

Yield: 4½ dozen 3-inch
cookies

M&M Cookies

One of my fondest memories of visiting my Aunt Cordelia was her large glass cookie jar filled with endless amounts of these cookies. Similar to chocolate-chip cookies, these are more fun because of all the colors.

1 cup plus 2 tablespoons all-purpose flour
½ teaspoon baking soda
½ teaspoon salt
½ cup butter, softened
½ cup firmly packed light-brown sugar

¼ cup granulated sugar
¾ teaspoon vanilla extract
1 egg
½ cup plain M&Ms, plus ½ cup more for decoration if desired

1 Preheat oven to 375° F. Prepare greased cookie sheets.

2 In a medium-sized bowl, stir together flour, baking soda, and salt.

3 In a large bowl, cream butter and sugars. Add vanilla and egg. Mix until well blended. Stir in flour mixture. Fold in M&Ms.

4 Drop by teaspoonfuls onto prepared cookie sheets. If desired, press extra M&Ms into tops of cookies before baking for extra color.

5 Bake for 12 to 15 minutes, until cookies are golden brown. Remove cookies to a wire rack to cool.

Yield: 3 dozen 2½-inch cookies

Brown Sugar Cookies

  This is a crunchy, butterscotch-flavored cookie.

2 cups all-purpose flour
½ teaspoon salt
½ teaspoon baking soda
½ cup butter

1 cup firmly packed dark-brown
   sugar
1 egg
1 teaspoon vanilla extract
¾ cup chopped pecans

---

1 Preheat oven to 350° F. Prepare greased cookie sheets.

2 In a large bowl, stir together flour, salt, and baking soda.

3 In another large bowl, cream butter and sugar. Add egg and vanilla; mix well. Stir in flour mixture and pecans. Drop by tablespoons onto prepared cookie sheets.

4 Bake for 12 to 14 minutes, until cookies feel firm in center. Remove cookies to a wire rack to cool.

Yield: 40 cookies

Oatmeal-Raisin Cookies

We can never have enough of these chewy, buttery cookies in the summer. They are my second-biggest seller and my husband's favorite!

3 cups quick-cooking rolled oats
1¼ cups all-purpose flour
½ teaspoon baking soda
¾ teaspoon salt
¾ cup butter, softened
1 cup firmly packed dark-brown sugar

½ cup granulated sugar
1 egg
¼ cup milk
1 teaspoon vanilla extract
1 cup raisins

1 Preheat oven to 350° F. Prepare greased cookie sheets.

2 In a large bowl, stir together oats, flour, baking soda, and salt.

3 In another large bowl, cream butter, sugars, egg, milk, and vanilla. Add oatmeal-flour mixture. Do not overmix. Fold in raisins. Drop by tablespoons onto prepared baking sheets 2 inches apart.

4 Bake for 12 minutes, until cookies are golden brown. Remove cookies to a wire rack to cool.

Yield: forty 2½-inch
cookies

Molasses Cookies

My Dad used to make these old-fashioned, cakey cookies for us when we were children. I think he used us as an excuse so that he could gobble them up, too!

5 cups all-purpose flour
1 teaspoon baking soda
¾ teaspoon salt
2 teaspoons ground ginger
1 teaspoon ground cinnamon
½ teaspoon ground cloves

1 cup molasses
2 cups granulated sugar
1 cup butter, softened
1 egg
1 cup milk

1 Preheat oven to 350° F. Prepare greased cookie sheets.

2 In a large bowl, stir together flour, baking soda, salt, ginger, cinnamon, and cloves.

3 In another large bowl, cream molasses, sugar, and butter. Mix in egg and milk. Stir in all dry ingredients and mix thoroughly. Using two tablespoons, drop onto prepared cookie sheets 2 inches apart.

4 Bake for 10 to 12 minutes, until center springs back to touch. Remove cookies to a wire rack to cool.

Yield: 6 dozen 3-inch
cookies

Ginger Hearts

At Christmastime, I can't keep my Mom away from these chewy, spicy cutout cookies. They are her absolute favorite and mine, too! This recipe also can be made into gingerbread men.

2½ cups all-purpose flour
1 tablespoon baking powder
¼ teaspoon baking soda
½ teaspoon salt
¼ teaspoon ground allspice
1 tablespoon ground cinnamon

1 teaspoon ground ginger
1 teaspoon ground cloves
1 egg
1 cup firmly packed dark-brown
  sugar
⅔ cup dark molasses
½ cup butter, softened

---

1 Preheat oven to 350° F.

2 In a large bowl, stir together flour, baking powder, baking soda, salt, and spices.

3 In another large bowl, beat egg and brown sugar. Add molasses and butter. Mix well. Add all dry ingredients and mix until combined. Roll dough into a ball and chill for ½ hour to 1 hour.

4 Prepare greased cookie sheets. Roll dough ¼ inch thick on a lightly floured board and cut with a 2-inch heart-shaped cookie cutter that has been dipped in flour. Place hearts 1½ inches apart on prepared cookie sheets.

5 Bake for 10 minutes, until slightly firm to touch (do *not* let edges brown). Don't overbake or cookies will be very hard. Remove cookies to a wire rack to cool.

Yield: fifty-three 2-inch
hearts

Polish Tea Cookies

*"Grandma" Esposito is the best cook I know. Years ago
I used to work at her daughter and son-in-law's
appliance repair shop answering the telephone. The
office was right off the kitchen, and every Christmas the
counters would be overflowing with these fantastic,
buttery cookies. They are very pretty, and if you want
to get really festive, you can fill some with green mint
jelly and others with raspberry jelly or jam. My favorite
filling is apricot.*

½ cup butter, softened
½ cup granulated sugar
1 egg yolk (reserve the white)
1 teaspoon vanilla extract

1 cup all-purpose flour
1½ cups chopped walnuts
1 egg white
Jelly or jam of choice

1 Preheat oven to 325° F. Prepare greased cookie sheets.

2 In a large bowl, cream butter and sugar slightly. Add egg yolk and
vanilla and mix well. Stir in flour.

3 Roll dough into small balls, the size of large marbles. Place chopped
walnuts on a piece of waxed paper. Dip balls in unbeaten egg white and
roll in chopped nuts. Place on prepared cookie sheets 1½ inches apart
and push down the center of each ball with your thumb.

4 Bake for 5 minutes, remove sheets from oven, and press down the
centers again with the back of a teaspoon. Bake for 20 minutes more, till
golden brown.

5 While still warm, fill with your favorite jam or jelly. These cookies
can be frozen just after rolling them in nuts. To defrost, just place balls
on cookie sheets until soft enough to press down centers.

Yield: 27 cookies

Butter Balls

My friend Dani gave me this recipe when we were kids.
These cookies have turned out to be one of my biggest
sellers at Christmastime.

1 cup butter, softened
4 tablespoons confectioners' sugar
1 teaspoon almond extract

2 cups all-purpose flour
¾ cup ground walnuts
¾ cup confectioners' sugar

1 In a large bowl, cream butter. Add the 4 tablespoons of sugar and the almond extract. Beat until creamy. Mix in flour and ground walnuts.

2 Roll dough into one large ball, wrap, and chill for several hours.

3 Preheat oven to 375° F. Prepare greased cookie sheets.

4 Roll dough into small balls and place 1 inch apart on prepared cookie sheets.

5 Bake for 20 minutes, or until tops are slightly cracked and bottoms are golden brown. Cool on wire racks and toss in confectioners' sugar. (These cookies freeze well unbaked. When you need them, just line them up on a greased cookie sheet, thaw, and bake.)

Yield: 4 dozen cookies

Shortbread

I studied in England for six months as an exchange student at Thomas Danby College. I wasn't crazy about most English baked goods, but their shortbread and scones are the best. This shortbread recipe has only three ingredients, but it took me a long time to figure out the exact proportions of each.

3 cups all-purpose flour
¾ cup granulated sugar

1½ cups cold butter, cut into 16 pieces

1 Preheat oven to 325° F.

2 In a large bowl, mix flour and sugar. Add cold butter pieces and work them into the flour-sugar mixture with your hands. When well combined and smooth, press mixture into an ungreased 13- by 9-inch pan.

3 Bake for 1 hour, or until golden brown in center and on edges. Cut into squares while still warm. (These cookies freeze well and can also be mailed to friends and family.)

Yield: thirty-two 2-inch
squares

Walnut Meringue Bars

This is a sweet, gooey bar for walnut lovers!

1½ cups all-purpose flour
1 teaspoon baking powder
½ cup butter, softened
¾ cup granulated sugar
2 egg yolks (reserve whites)

2 tablespoons milk
1 teaspoon vanilla extract
2 egg whites
½ cup firmly packed dark-brown
   sugar
1 cup chopped walnuts

1 Preheat oven to 350° F. Grease a 9-inch square pan.

2 In a medium-sized bowl, stir together flour and baking powder.

3 In a large bowl, cream butter and sugar. Add egg yolks one at a time. Beat until light and fluffy. Alternately add flour mixture and milk to butter mixture. Add vanilla and beat again. Scrape batter into prepared pan and spread evenly.

4 Bake for 20 minutes; remove from oven.

5 Meanwhile, beat egg whites until stiff while gradually adding brown sugar, beating well after each addition. Fold in walnuts.

6 Spread mixture evenly over baked cookies and bake for 20 minutes longer, or till golden brown. Cut into bars while still warm.

Yield: 16 bars

Chunkies

These cookies have a wonderful, wholesome look. They are very rich and are full of flavor and texture.

1¼ cups all-purpose flour
½ teaspoon salt
½ teaspoon baking soda
½ cup butter
½ cup firmly packed dark-brown sugar
¼ cup granulated sugar

1 teaspoon vanilla extract
1 egg
1 cup semisweet chocolate chips
1 cup raisins
1 cup chopped walnuts

1 Preheat oven to 350° F. Prepare greased cookie sheets.

2 In a medium-sized bowl, stir together flour, salt, and baking soda.

3 In a large bowl, cream butter and sugars. Add vanilla and egg. Mix. Stir in flour mixture. Stir in chocolate chips, raisins, and walnuts. Drop, about 2 inches apart, onto prepared cookie sheets using two tablespoons.

4 Bake for 12 minutes, or until golden brown. Remove cookies to a wire rack to cool.

Yield: thirty-six 2-inch
cookies

Lemon Bars

This recent addition to the bake shop's menu has turned out to be a big seller. These bars are very rich and buttery with a tart lemon top. While testing this recipe, we added more lemon juice each night until we got the perfect balance. The usual response from my bakers was, "More lemon!" My husband and I love to eat these after they have been in the freezer for about half an hour. They are very refreshing in the summer.

Bars

¾ cup butter, softened
1½ cups all-purpose flour

⅓ cup granulated sugar

Topping

4 eggs
5 tablespoons all-purpose flour

2 cups granulated sugar
¾ cup fresh lemon juice

---

1 Preheat oven to 350° F.

2 *To make bars:* Mix butter, flour, and sugar until combined. Press mixture into the bottom of a 13- by 9-inch ungreased pan. Bake for 20 minutes, or until just turning brown.

3 *To make topping:* Lightly whisk eggs. In a separate bowl, mix flour and sugar together. With a wooden spoon, gently stir the flour mixture into the eggs.

4 When you are ready to pour the topping onto the shortbread base, add lemon juice, stir, and pour mixture immediately over shortbread.

5 Bake for 20 minutes more, or until topping is firm to touch. Cool before cutting.

Yield: thirty-two 2-inch
squares

Muffins

Banana–Coffee Cake Muffins

This recipe was developed by one of my employees for
Family Circle *magazine. The combination of ingredients*
makes a flavorful, moist muffin.

2½ cups all-purpose flour
1 teaspoon baking powder
½ teaspoon baking soda
½ teaspoon salt
1 tablespoon instant-coffee powder
1 tablespoon hot water

1⅓ cups mashed fully ripe banana
1 cup butter, softened
1¼ cups granulated sugar
1 egg
1 cup semisweet chocolate chips

1 Preheat oven to 400° F. Grease twelve 3- by 1½-inch muffin cups.

2 In a large bowl, stir together flour, baking powder, baking soda, and salt.

3 In a separate bowl, combine instant-coffee powder and water. Stir into bananas; reserve.

4 In a large bowl, cream butter and sugar until light and fluffy. Beat in egg. Mix in banana mixture. Stir in flour mixture. Fold in chocolate chips. Divide batter evenly into prepared muffin cups.

5 Bake for 25 to 30 minutes, or until a cake tester inserted in center of one muffin comes out clean. Remove muffins from tins and cool on a wire rack.

Yield: 12 muffins

Orange–Poppy Seed Muffins

Try these if you like a very light and moist muffin.

1¼ cups all-purpose flour
1¼ teaspoons baking powder
½ teaspoon baking soda
¼ teaspoon salt
½ cup butter, softened
¾ cup granulated sugar

2 eggs, separated
1 tablespoon freshly grated orange
   rind
1 teaspoon vanilla extract
½ cup buttermilk
2 tablespoons poppy seeds

1 Preheat oven to 400° F. Grease nine 3- by 1½-inch muffin cups.

2 In a medium-sized bowl, stir together flour, baking powder, baking soda, and salt.

3 In a large bowl, cream butter and sugar until light and fluffy. Add egg yolks one at a time, beating well after each addition. Beat in the orange rind and vanilla.

4 Add flour mixture and buttermilk alternately to the butter mixture. Fold in the poppy seeds. Beat egg whites to soft peaks and fold into flour mixture. Spoon batter into prepared muffin cups, filling them to the top.

5 Bake for 20 minutes, or until a cake tester inserted in center of one muffin comes out clean.

Yield: 9 muffins

Corn Muffins

While participating in the Hotel/Motel Show in Manhattan, I met a model at the booth next to mine. She said her favorite thing to bake was her Mom's corn muffins. I had been searching for years for the perfect corn muffin, so in trade I offered her a strawberry-rhubarb pie recipe. She copied down the recipe, and I ended up with the best corn-muffin recipe ever! Note: Our baker, Michelle Strazzere, changed this recipe by adding half-and-half instead of the milk—and they were even better! I'll leave that choice to you.

1 cup all-purpose flour
1 cup cornmeal
½ cup granulated sugar
1 tablespoon baking powder

½ teaspoon salt
½ cup butter, softened
1 cup milk or half-and-half
1 egg, lightly beaten

1 Preheat oven to 400° F. Grease nine 3- by 1½-inch muffin cups.

2 In a large bowl, stir together flour, cornmeal, sugar, baking powder, and salt. Add butter and mix until crumbly.

3 In a separate bowl, mix milk and egg. Fold liquid mixture into flour mixture. Spoon mixture evenly into prepared muffin cups, filling them to the top.

4 Bake for 25 minutes, or until a cake tester inserted in center of one muffin comes out clean. They will not get very brown on top.

Yield: 9 muffins

Toasted Coconut
Muffins

This recipe makes a very moist and buttery muffin.

1 cup sweetened coconut
1 cup old-fashioned rolled oats
1 cup buttermilk
1 cup all-purpose flour
½ teaspoon salt

½ teaspoon baking soda
1½ teaspoons baking powder
½ cup butter, melted
1 egg
½ cup firmly packed dark-brown
    sugar

1 Preheat oven to 350° F. Spread coconut on a cookie sheet and toast in oven for 10 minutes, tossing every few minutes.

2 Combine oats and buttermilk in a small bowl. Let soak for 30 minutes.

3 Preheat oven to 400° F. Grease ten 3- by 1½-inch muffin cups.

4 In a large bowl, stir together flour, salt, baking soda, baking powder, and coconut.

5 In a separate bowl, combine melted butter, egg, and brown sugar. Add oat mixture to butter mixture. Fold in dry ingredients. Spoon mixture evenly into prepared muffin cups, filling them to the top.

6 Bake for 20 minutes, or until a cake tester inserted in center of one muffin comes out clean. Remove muffin tin(s) to wire rack. Cool 5 minutes before removing muffins from cups; finish cooling on rack.

Yield: 10 muffins

Blueberry Muffins

These are loaded with blueberries and are so buttery that they don't need to be served with butter. These were our fastest-moving muffin until the oat-bran craze hit.

3 cups all-purpose flour
4½ teaspoons baking powder
½ teaspoon baking soda
1¼ cups granulated sugar
½ teaspoon salt

1 cup butter
1¼ cups milk
2 eggs, lightly beaten
2 cups fresh or frozen blueberries

1 Preheat oven to 400° F. Grease twelve 3- by 1½-inch muffin cups.

2 In a large bowl, stir together flour, baking powder, baking soda, sugar, and salt.

3 In a medium-sized saucepan, melt butter. Add milk and lightly beaten egg.

4 Add butter mixture to dry ingredients and mix lightly just until moistened. Fold in blueberries. Spoon mixture evenly into prepared muffin cups.

5 Bake for 25 to 30 minutes, or until a cake tester inserted in center of one muffin comes out clean.

Yield: 12 muffins

Bran Muffins

These are dense, moist, and hearty muffins. They were very popular at the bake shop, but we replaced them with oat-bran muffins.

1½ cups wheat bran
1¼ cups milk
1½ cups all-purpose flour
1 teaspoon salt
1 tablespoon baking powder
⅓ cup granulated sugar

1 teaspoon ground cinnamon
¼ teaspoon ground cloves
½ cup butter
¼ cup molasses
1 egg, lightly beaten
½ cup raisins

1 Preheat oven to 400° F. Grease eleven 3- by 1½-inch muffin cups.

2 In a large bowl, combine bran and milk and let stand for 10 minutes.

3 In another large bowl, stir together flour, salt, baking powder, sugar, cinnamon, and cloves.

4 In a medium-sized saucepan, melt butter. Add molasses and egg. Add butter mixture to bran mixture. Stir in flour mixture. Fold in raisins. Spoon batter evenly into prepared muffin cups.

5 Bake for 20 to 25 minutes, or until a cake tester inserted in center of one muffin comes out clean.

Yield: 11 muffins

Prune Muffins

Moist, sweet prunes with a hint of orange give these muffins a spicy flavor.

1 cup all-purpose flour
½ cup whole-wheat flour
½ cup quick-cooking rolled oats
1 tablespoon baking powder
½ teaspoon salt
1 teaspoon ground cinnamon

1 tablespoon grated orange rind
½ cup butter
⅓ cup brown sugar
1 egg, lightly beaten
½ cup milk
1¼ cups chopped prunes

1 Preheat oven to 400° F. Grease ten 3- by 1½-inch muffin cups.

2 In a large bowl, stir together flours, oats, baking powder, salt, cinnamon, and orange rind.

3 In another large bowl, cream butter and sugar. Beat in egg and then milk. Add prunes and mix well. Add flour mixture and mix lightly. Spoon batter evenly into prepared muffin cups.

4 Bake for 20 minutes, or until a cake tester inserted in center of one muffin comes out clean. Remove muffin tin(s) to wire rack. Cool 5 minutes before removing muffins from cups; finish cooling on rack.

Yield: 10 muffins

Apple-Raisin
Bran Muffins

My sister Karin makes these in her upstate New York home during apple season. Each muffin is a meal in itself!

1½ cups all-purpose flour
1 cup wheat bran
½ cup firmly packed dark-brown
    sugar
1 tablespoon baking powder
½ teaspoon salt
1 teaspoon ground cinnamon
½ cup butter

1 cup buttermilk
1 teaspoon vanilla extract
¼ cup molasses
1 egg
1 cup peeled, cored, and chopped
    apples
½ cup raisins
½ cup chopped walnuts

1 Preheat oven to 400° F. Grease twelve 3- by 1½-inch muffin cups.

2 Combine dry ingredients in a large bowl.

3 In a medium-sized saucepan, melt butter and add buttermilk, vanilla, molasses, and egg. Stir the liquid mixture into the dry ingredients and mix until just moistened. Fold in apples, raisins, and walnuts. Spoon mixture evenly into prepared muffin cups.

4 Bake for 20 to 25 minutes, or until a cake tester inserted in center of one muffin comes out clean. Remove muffin tin(s) to wire rack. Cool 5 minutes before removing muffins from cups; finish cooling on rack.

Yield: 12 muffins

Cranberry-Oatmeal Muffins

These are hearty muffins, studded with tart red cranberries.

¾ cup all-purpose flour
¾ cup whole-wheat flour
1 cup old-fashioned rolled oats
½ cup firmly packed dark-brown
    sugar
1 tablespoon baking powder
¾ teaspoon salt

1 teaspoon ground cinnamon
½ cup butter
½ cup milk
1 egg, lightly beaten
1 cup chopped cranberries
½ cup chopped walnuts

---

1 Preheat oven to 400° F. Grease eleven 3- by 1½-inch muffin cups.

2 In a large bowl, combine all dry ingredients.

3 In a saucepan, melt butter and add milk and lightly beaten egg. Stir the butter mixture into the dry ingredients. Fold in cranberries and walnuts. Spoon mixture evenly into prepared muffin cups.

4 Bake for 20 to 25 minutes, or until a cake tester inserted in center of one muffin comes out clean. Remove muffin tin(s) to wire rack. Cool 5 minutes before removing muffins from cups; finish cooling on rack.

Yield: 11 muffins

Lemon Muffins

After one customer raved about his own lemon muffins, he shared the recipe with me. These muffins are not too sweet and are nice and lemony. They're delicious toasted, with butter!

2 cups all-purpose flour
½ cup granulated sugar
1 tablespoon baking powder
1 teaspoon salt
½ cup butter

½ cup fresh lemon juice
2 tablespoons grated lemon rind
2 eggs, lightly beaten
Granulated sugar (optional)

1 Preheat oven to 400° F. Grease ten 3- by 1½-inch muffin cups.

2 In a large bowl, combine flour, sugar, baking powder, and salt.

3 In a small saucepan, melt butter. Add lemon juice and rind and eggs. Fold butter mixture into dry ingredients. Spoon mixture evenly into prepared muffin cups. Sprinkle tops with granulated sugar if desired.

4 Bake for 15 to 20 minutes, or until a cake tester inserted in center of one muffin comes out clean.

Yield: 10 muffins

Orange-Pineapple Muffins

These muffins are light and moist, with hidden bits of pineapple and a hint of orange. Make them on a wintry day and they will remind you of springtime.

3 cups all-purpose flour
½ teaspoon salt
1 tablespoon baking powder
¼ teaspoon baking soda
½ cup butter
1 cup granulated sugar

2 eggs
1 teaspoon vanilla extract
1 cup orange-pineapple juice
¾ cup crushed, drained pineapple
1 tablespoon grated orange rind

1 Preheat oven to 400° F. Grease fifteen 3- by 1½-inch muffin cups.

2 In a large bowl, stir together flour, salt, baking powder, and baking soda.

3 In another large bowl, cream butter and sugar until light and fluffy. Beat in eggs, one at a time. Add vanilla to the juice. Stir flour mixture into butter mixture alternately with juice mixture, beginning and ending with flour mixture. Fold in crushed pineapple and grated orange rind. Spoon mixture evenly into prepared muffin cups, filling each cup to the top.

4 Bake for 20 minutes, or until a cake tester inserted in center of one muffin comes out clean.

Yield: 15 muffins

Brownie Muffins

Very light, these are a favorite among my friends.

1 cup all-purpose flour
1¼ cups granulated sugar
¼ teaspoon salt
1 tablespoon baking powder
1 cup butter

4 squares (4 ounces) sweet baking
   chocolate
4 eggs, lightly beaten
1 teaspoon vanilla extract
1 cup chopped pecans

---

1 Preheat oven to 400° F. Grease sixteen 3- by 1½-inch muffin cups.

2 In a large bowl, stir together flour, sugar, salt, and baking powder.

3 In a small saucepan, melt butter and chocolate over low heat. Stir chocolate mixture into flour mixture. Add eggs and vanilla and whisk just until ingredients are evenly moistened. Fold in pecans. Spoon the batter evenly into prepared muffin cups, filling each cup three-quarters full.

4 Bake for 20 minutes, or until springy to the touch.

Yield: 16 muffins

Cranberry-Nut
Muffins

These muffins are full of moist, tart cranberries surrounded by the sweetness of buttery cake and crunchy walnuts.

2 cups all-purpose flour
1 tablespoon baking powder
¼ teaspoon salt
⅔ cup granulated sugar
½ cup butter

1 cup orange juice
1 egg, lightly beaten
1 cup chopped cranberries
1 cup chopped walnuts
1 tablespoon grated orange rind

---

1 Preheat oven to 400° F. Grease eleven 3- by 1½-inch muffin cups.

2 In a large bowl, stir together flour, baking powder, salt, and sugar.

3 Melt butter in a saucepan over low heat. Add orange juice and egg. Stir butter mixture into flour mixture. Fold in cranberries, walnuts, and orange rind. Spoon batter evenly into prepared muffin cups.

4 Bake for 25 to 30 minutes, or until a cake tester inserted in center of one muffin comes out clean. Remove muffin tin(s) to wire rack. Cool 5 minutes before removing muffins from cups; finish cooling on rack.

Yield: 11 muffins

Coffee-Pecan Muffins

These muffins are a hearty treat for coffee lovers! They are best served warm.

1¾ cups all-purpose flour
½ cup firmly packed dark-brown sugar
1 tablespoon baking powder
¼ teaspoon salt
¾ cup milk

2 tablespoons instant coffee powder
1 teaspoon vanilla extract
½ cup butter, melted
1 egg, lightly beaten
1 cup chopped pecans

1 Preheat oven to 400° F. Grease nine 3- by 1½-inch muffin cups.

2 In a large bowl, stir together flour, brown sugar, baking powder, and salt.

3 In a medium-sized bowl, combine milk, instant coffee powder, vanilla, butter, and egg. Let stand for 5 minutes.

4 Add milk-butter mixture to the flour mixture and mix lightly. Fold in pecans. Spoon batter evenly into prepared muffin cups.

5 Bake for 20 minutes, or until a cake tester inserted in center of one muffin comes out clean. Remove muffin tin(s) to wire rack. Cool 5 minutes before removing muffins from cups; finish cooling on rack.

Yield: 9 muffins

Sweet-Potato Muffins

Serve these at breakfast or as a change of pace from ordinary dinner rolls.

1½ cups all-purpose flour
¼ cup firmly packed dark-brown
   sugar
1 tablespoon baking powder
½ teaspoon salt
1 teaspoon ground cinnamon
¼ teaspoon ground nutmeg
½ cup butter, melted

½ cup milk
1 egg, lightly beaten
1 cup cooked and mashed sweet
   potato
½ cup dried fruit: figs, dates, or
   raisins

1 Preheat oven to 400° F. Grease eleven 3- by 1½-inch muffin cups.

2 In a large bowl, stir together flour, brown sugar, baking powder, salt, cinnamon, and nutmeg.

3 In a separate bowl, beat together butter, milk, egg, and sweet potato. Combine butter mixture with flour mixture. Mix lightly. Fold in dried fruit. Spoon mixture evenly into prepared muffin cups.

4 Bake for 20 to 25 minutes, or until springy to the touch.

Yield: 11 muffins

Banana Muffins

These are a great alternative to a heavier banana bread. The wheat germ adds a nice, wholesome flavor.

2 cups all-purpose flour
½ cup wheat germ
1 tablespoon baking powder
½ teaspoon baking soda
½ teaspoon salt

½ cup butter
½ cup honey
1 teaspoon vanilla extract
2 cups mashed, fully ripe banana

1 Preheat oven to 400° F. Grease twelve 3- by 1½-inch muffin cups.

2 In a large bowl, stir together flour, wheat germ, baking powder, baking soda, and salt.

3 In a medium-sized saucepan, melt butter. Add honey, vanilla, and mashed banana. Add butter mixture to flour mixture and mix lightly. Spoon mixture evenly into prepared muffin cups.

4 Bake for 20 minutes, or until a cake tester inserted in center of one muffin comes out clean.

Yield: 12 muffins

Pumpkin Muffins

These moist and spicy muffins are wonderful served on a cold fall morning with your favorite tea.

2 cups all-purpose flour
½ cup firmly packed dark-brown
   sugar
1½ teaspoons baking powder
¼ teaspoon baking soda
1 teaspoon ground cinnamon
½ teaspoon ground cloves
¼ teaspoon ground nutmeg
1 cup mashed fresh pumpkin, *or* 1
   (8 ounce) can solid-packed
   pumpkin (not pumpkin pie
   filling)

½ cup butter, melted
¼ cup plain yogurt
2 eggs, lightly beaten
¼ cup maple syrup
1 teaspoon vanilla extract
¾ cup raisins
¾ cup chopped walnuts

1 Preheat oven to 400° F. Grease twelve 3- by 1½-inch muffin cups.

2 In a large bowl, stir together flour, sugar, baking powder, baking soda, and spices.

3 In another large bowl, combine pumpkin, butter, yogurt, eggs, maple syrup, and vanilla. Fold dry ingredients into pumpkin mixture. Stir in raisins and walnuts. Spoon evenly into prepared muffin cups.

4 Bake for 25 to 30 minutes, or until a cake tester inserted in center of one muffin comes out clean. Remove tin(s) to wire rack. Cool 5 minutes before removing muffins from cups; finish cooling on rack.

Yield: 12 muffins

Yeast Breads
and Quick Breads

Shredded-Wheat Bread

My grandmother won second prize at the Southampton Historical Society Annual Fair in 1963 with this recipe. This loaf keeps a long time and makes great toast.

2¾ cups boiling water
3 large Shredded-Wheat biscuits
1 tablespoon salt
2 tablespoons butter

½ cup molasses
1 package dry yeast
¼ cup warm water
8 cups all-purpose flour

1 In a large bowl, pour boiling water over biscuits. Add salt, butter, and molasses. Cool to lukewarm.

2 Dissolve yeast in warm water and add to cooled molasses mixture. Add flour until dough is soft and can be easily kneaded. Knead dough on a lightly floured board until it is smooth and elastic.

3 Form dough into a large ball and place it in a well-oiled bowl. Cover bowl with plastic wrap and let rise until doubled in bulk.

4 Punch down dough and turn it out onto a lightly floured board. Knead lightly and divide into three equal portions. Shape into loaves and place each in a greased 9- by 5- by 3-inch loaf pan. Let rise until doubled in bulk.

5 Bake in a preheated 400° F. oven for 30 to 40 minutes, or until bread is brown and, when tapped on top, sounds hollow. Remove from pans and cool on wire racks. Freeze bread the same day it's made if you can't use it all at once.

Yield: 3 loaves

Peasant Bread

This is my favorite bread! The extra-thick crust makes this wonderful with soup and cheese.

1 package dry yeast
2¼ cups warm water
1 tablespoon granulated sugar

1½ tablespoons salt
6½ cups all-purpose flour

1 Dissolve yeast in warm water. Stir in sugar and salt. Mix well.

2 Add flour, 1 cup at a time. If dough gets too tough, knead in the rest of the flour. When dough is smooth and elastic, knead for 5 to 8 minutes.

3 Grease the inside of a large bowl; place dough in bowl, and cover bowl with plastic wrap. Let dough rise in a warm place until doubled in bulk.

4 Punch down dough and turn it out onto a lightly floured board. Cut into two equal portions and form into balls. Make an **X** on the top of each loaf and place on a cookie sheet sprinkled with cornmeal. Let rest for 5 minutes.

5 Brush loaves with water and place in a cold oven. Place a small pan of boiling water in bottom of oven. Turn on oven to 400° F. and bake for 45 minutes, or until brown (an electric oven may take longer than a gas oven). Cool on wire racks. Best served warm.

Yield: 2 loaves

Anadama Bread

My grandmother used to bring steaming-hot loaves of this cornmeal-molasses bread to our home. The family would gather around our butcher-block table, cut off slabs of the bread, and spread them with butter and apricot jam. Usually by the time my grandmother left to go home, the bread had already disappeared!

2 cups boiling water
½ cup cornmeal
2 tablespoons butter
½ cup molasses

1 tablespoon salt
2 packages dry yeast
½ cup warm water
7 to 8 cups all-purpose flour

1 Pour boiling water into a large bowl, then stir in the cornmeal. Add butter, molasses, and salt. Cool to lukewarm.

2 Sprinkle yeast into one-half cup warm water and stir until dissolved. Add this to the cooled cornmeal mixture. Add enough flour to make a stiff dough and knead on a lightly floured board until smooth and elastic.

3 Place dough in a greased bowl and brush the top lightly with oil. Cover bowl with plastic wrap and let rise until doubled in bulk.

4 Punch down dough and turn it out onto a lightly floured board. Divide dough into two equal pieces. Shape each into a loaf and place in a greased 9- by 5- by 3-inch pan. Brush each loaf with oil and cover pans with plastic wrap.

5 Let rise again until doubled in bulk and bake in a preheated 375° F. oven for 40 to 50 minutes, or until loaves sound hollow when tapped with your finger. Remove bread immediately from pans and cool on wire rack.

Yield: 2 loaves

Swedish Limpa Bread

When my grandmother was nineteen, she moved to the United States from Sweden. She brought this recipe with her, and it is still one of her favorites. This loaf is heavy and full of flavor. It's great toasted!

3½ cups all-purpose flour
1 package dry yeast
1 teaspoon granulated sugar
1¼ cups milk
¾ cup warm water
½ cup molasses
¼ cup firmly packed dark-brown
    sugar

3 tablespoons butter
2 teaspoons caraway seeds
1 teaspoon anise seeds
1 tablespoon salt
2 tablespoons grated orange rind
4 to 5 cups rye flour

1 In a large bowl, stir together all-purpose flour, yeast, and sugar.

2 In a saucepan, heat milk, water, molasses, brown sugar, and butter until combined. Add seeds, salt, and orange rind, and cool to lukewarm.

3 Add liquid ingredients to flour mixture and mix well. Gradually add enough rye flour to make a stiff dough. Knead until smooth and elastic.

4 Form dough into a ball and place in a large oiled bowl. Cover bowl with plastic wrap and let rise in a warm place until doubled in bulk.

5 Punch down dough, remove from bowl, divide into two equal portions, and form into balls. Shape each one into a loaf. Either place dough in a greased 9- by 5- by 3-inch loaf pan, or form into a 12-inch log and place on a greased cookie sheet. Make four diagonal slashes on top. Let rise until doubled in bulk.

6 Bake in a preheated oven at 375° F. for 35 to 45 minutes or until bread sounds hollow when tapped with your finger.

Yield: 2 loaves

No-Knead
Oatmeal Bread

A friend of my Mom's, Dot Nugent, once brought two loaves of this sweet and chewy bread to our home as a gift. They lasted less than a day, so I got the recipe, and it has been my brother's favorite for years.

1 cup firmly packed dark-brown
    sugar
1 tablespoon salt
1¾ cups old-fashioned rolled oats
3 cups boiling water

2 tablespoons butter
1 package dry yeast
¼ cup warm water
6 cups all-purpose flour

1 In a large bowl, stir together sugar, salt, and oats. Add boiling water and butter; let stand until lukewarm.

2 Sprinkle yeast into ¼ cup warm water and stir until dissolved. Add yeast mixture to oat mixture. Stir in flour 1 cup at a time. Dough will be sticky.

3 Transfer to a greased bowl, cover bowl with plastic wrap, and let rise until doubled in bulk. Lift and drop dough into bowl three or four times.

4 Grease two 9- by 5- by 3-inch loaf pans and divide dough into two equal portions. Cover with a towel and let rise until doubled in bulk.

5 Bake in a preheated oven at 450° F. for 10 minutes. Lower oven to 350° F. and bake for another 45 minutes, or until bread sounds hollow when tapped with your finger. Remove bread immediately from pans and cool on wire racks.

Yield: 2 loaves

French Bread

 This traditional loaf can accompany any meal.

1 package dry yeast
1¼ cups warm water

3 to 3½ cups all-purpose flour
2 teaspoons salt

---

1 In a large bowl, stir yeast into ¼ cup of the warm water. Let stand for 10 minutes.

2 Beat in the remaining 1 cup warm water, 2 cups of the flour, and the salt. Beat until well combined. Add the remaining flour and knead until smooth and elastic.

3 Form the dough into a ball and place in a well-oiled bowl. Cover bowl with plastic wrap and let rise until doubled in bulk.

4 Punch down dough and let it rise again until doubled in bulk. Punch down dough again and lightly knead it on a lightly floured board for 1 to 2 minutes. Divide dough into two equal portions and let rest for 5 minutes.

5 Form each piece into a rope as long as your sheet pan and place on a cookie sheet that has been sprinkled lightly with cornmeal. Let loaves rest for 30 minutes.

6 Bake in a preheated 450° F. oven for 20 minutes, or until crust is golden brown.

Yield: 2 loaves

White Bread

This will beat store-bought any day!

5½ cups all-purpose flour
3 tablespoons granulated sugar
2 teaspoons salt
1 package dry yeast
⅓ cup warm water

2 cups milk
3 tablespoons butter
1 egg yolk
1 tablespoon water

1 In a large bowl, stir together flour, sugar, and salt.

2 In a separate bowl, dissolve yeast in ⅓ cup warm water and set aside.

3 In a medium-sized saucepan, heat milk and butter until just warm. Add yeast mixture to milk mixture and pour liquid ingredients into flour mixture. Mix well and knead on a lightly floured board until smooth and elastic, at least 10 minutes.

4 Place dough in an oiled bowl, brush top with oil, and cover bowl with plastic wrap. Place in a draft-free place until doubled in bulk.

5 Punch down dough and divide into two equal pieces. Shape into two loaves and place in two greased 9- by 5- by 3-inch loaf pans. Cover bowl with plastic wrap, and let rise until doubled in bulk.

6 In a small bowl mix egg yolk and water, using a fork. Brush tops of loaves with egg mixture.

7 Bake at 375° F. for 30 minutes, or until golden brown. Remove bread immediately from pans and cool loaves on wire rack.

Yield: 2 loaves

Potato Bread

*This is my favorite white bread. It's very soft and is
perfect for peanut-butter sandwiches.*

1 package dry yeast
½ cup potato water, lukewarm
½ cup butter
½ cup granulated sugar
3 eggs
1 cup cooked and mashed potatoes
    (reserve cooking water)

1 tablespoon salt
1 cup milk, lukewarm
7 cups all-purpose flour
1 egg yolk
1 tablespoon water

1 Stir yeast into potato water until dissolved. Set aside.

2 In a large bowl, cream butter and sugar. Beat in eggs one at a time.
Add potatoes and yeast mixture. Add salt and milk and mix well. Add
flour 1 cup at a time until you have a stiff dough.

3 Turn out onto a lightly floured board and knead until smooth and
elastic. Put dough in an oiled bowl, cover with plastic wrap, and
refrigerate overnight.

4 Punch down dough and turn it out onto a lightly floured board.
Shape into three loaves of equal size. Place in greased 8½- by 4½- by
2½-inch loaf pans. Cover and let rise until doubled in bulk.

5 Make egg wash by beating together egg yolk and water. Brush lightly
on tops of loaves.

6 Preheat oven to 375° F.

7 Bake for 25 minutes, or until slightly golden. Cool on a wire rack.

Yield: 3 loaves

Cinnamon Swirl–
Sweet-Potato Bread

 *This bread is wonderful served warm and is also great
for making French toast.*

1½ cups milk
2 tablespoons granulated sugar
½ cup butter
1 tablespoon salt
1 cup mashed sweet potato
2 packages dry yeast

½ cup warm water
7½ cups all-purpose flour
1½ cups raisins
4 tablespoons butter, softened
½ cup granulated sugar
2 teaspoons ground cinnamon

1 In a small saucepan, scald milk. Add sugar, butter, and salt. Stir until butter melts, then add mashed sweet potato. Cool to lukewarm.

2 In a large bowl, dissolve yeast in ½ cup warm water. Add milk mixture and 4 cups flour. Beat with an electric mixer until smooth, about 2 minutes. Stir in raisins. Gradually add remaining flour, mixing until it forms a stiff dough.

3 Turn dough out onto a lightly floured board. Knead until smooth and elastic. Place in an oiled bowl and brush top with oil. Cover bowl with plastic wrap and let rise in a warm place until doubled in bulk.

4 Punch down dough and turn it out onto a lightly floured board. Divide into two equal portions and roll each one into a 16- by 8-inch rectangle. Spread 2 tablespoons of butter on each rectangle. Stir together sugar and cinnamon and sprinkle half on each rectangle.

5 Starting from the narrow side, roll up and pinch edges and ends together. Tuck ends under slightly. Place seam-side down in greased 9- by 5- by 3-inch loaf pans. Brush tops with melted butter, cover, and let rise until doubled in bulk.

6 Preheat oven to 375° F.

7 Bake for 35 to 40 minutes, or until loaves are golden brown and sound hollow when tapped with your finger. Remove bread immediately from pans and cool on a wire rack.

Yield: 2 loaves

Sweet Dinner Rolls

*Serve these right out of the oven with lots of fresh,
creamy butter.*

2 cups milk
½ cup butter
¼ cup granulated sugar
1¼ teaspoons salt
1 package yeast

¼ cup warm water
2 eggs
6 cups all-purpose flour
1 egg yolk
1 tablespoon water

1 In a medium-sized saucepan, scald milk. Add butter, sugar, and salt.
Cool to lukewarm.

2 Soften yeast in ¼ cup warm water until dissolved. Add yeast to milk
mixture. Beat in eggs. Gradually add flour. Knead dough until it is
smooth and elastic.

3 Place dough in an oiled bowl, brush top with oil, cover bowl with
plastic wrap, and let rise until doubled in bulk.

4 Punch down dough, remove from bowl, and cut into thirty-six equal
pieces. Shape each piece into a roll and place them on greased pans
about 1 inch apart from each other. Let rise until doubled in bulk.

5 Make egg wash: Mix egg yolk and water thoroughly. Brush tops of
the rolls with egg wash before putting in oven.

6 Bake in a preheated 425° F. oven for 20 to 25 minutes, or until
golden brown. Serve warm.

Yield: 36 dinner rolls

Squash Rolls

My sister-in-law, Robin King, brought this recipe to our family from her home in Connecticut. These rolls are very light and slightly sweet. I love to serve them with chicken or fish because of their beautiful, soft orange color.

1 package dry yeast
¼ cup warm water
½ cup milk
½ cup cooked and mashed
    butternut squash

⅓ cup granulated sugar
1 teaspoon salt
4 tablespoons butter
2½ to 2¾ cups all-purpose flour

1 Dissolve yeast in ¼ cup warm water. Set aside.

2 In a 1-quart saucepan, scald milk; add squash, sugar, salt, and butter. Add yeast mixture.

3 In a large bowl, add squash mixture to flour and mix well. On a lightly floured board, knead until dough is smooth and elastic.

4 Put dough in an oiled bowl, cover bowl with plastic wrap, and let rise until doubled in bulk.

5 Punch down dough and turn it out onto a lightly floured board. Cut into twelve equal portions and form into rolls. Place rolls side by side in a greased 9- by 13-inch pan. Cover and let rise until doubled in bulk.

6 Bake in a preheated 350° F. oven for 20 minutes, or until crust is golden brown.

Yield: 12 rolls

Irish Soda Bread

This quick, easy bread is perfect served warm for breakfast or dinner.

4 cups all-purpose flour
2 tablespoons granulated sugar
1 tablespoon baking powder
1 teaspoon baking soda
1 teaspoon salt

½ cup butter
1 cup raisins
3 tablespoons caraway seeds
2 cups buttermilk

1 Preheat oven to 375° F. Lightly grease a large cookie sheet.

2 In a large bowl, stir together flour, sugar, baking powder, baking soda, and salt. Using a pastry blender or fork, cut in butter until mixture resembles coarse meal. Add raisins and caraway seeds and toss lightly. Add buttermilk and toss mixture with a fork until all dry ingredients are moistened. Dough will be very soft.

3 Form dough into a ball and lightly knead on a floured board for about 30 seconds or until dough is smooth. Divide dough into two equal portions and shape into balls. Place them on the cookie sheet and, with a sharp knife, cut an **X** on top of each loaf about ¼-inch deep.

4 Bake for 50 minutes, or until crusty and golden.

Yield: 2 loaves

Zucchini Bread

What a great way to use up all those overgrown zucchini from the garden! The crushed pineapple adds a special touch to an otherwise common loaf.

3 cups all-purpose flour
1 teaspoon baking powder
1 teaspoon baking soda
½ teaspoon salt
1 tablespoon ground cinnamon
3 eggs

1½ cups granulated sugar
2 teaspoons vanilla extract
1 cup vegetable oil
3 cups grated zucchini
1 cup crushed and drained
    pineapple
1 cup chopped walnuts

1 Preheat oven to 350° F. Grease a 9- by 5- by 3-inch loaf pan.

2 In a large bowl, stir together flour, baking powder, baking soda, salt, and cinnamon.

3 In another large bowl, beat together eggs, sugar, vanilla, and oil. Add zucchini and mix well. Add flour mixture and stir. Stir in pineapple and walnuts. Pour batter into prepared pan.

4 Bake for 50 to 60 minutes, or until loaf springs back when lightly touched.

Yield: 1 loaf

Banana-Nut Bread

*My friend Anne Marie Astorr-Clark gave me this recipe
years ago. It has always been a favorite of mine because
it is loaded with bananas and is very moist
and dense.*

4 cups all-purpose flour
4 teaspoons baking powder
½ teaspoon baking soda
1 teaspoon salt
¾ cup butter

1⅓ cups granulated sugar
4 eggs
4½ cups fully ripe mashed bananas
2 cups chopped walnuts

1 Preheat oven to 350° F. Grease two 9- by 5- by 3-inch loaf pans.

2 In a large bowl, stir together flour, baking powder, baking soda, and salt.

3 In another large bowl, cream butter and sugar. Add eggs and beat well. Add dry ingredients alternately with mashed bananas to butter mixture. Fold in nuts. Pour batter evenly into prepared pans.

4 Bake for 1 hour, or until a cake tester inserted in center comes out clean.

Yield: 2 large loaves

Scones

When I studied in England I used to eat these every day. They are like a very rich tea biscuit. Plan to serve them right out of the oven since cold scones offer no comparison.

4 cups all-purpose flour
2 tablespoons baking powder
½ teaspoon salt
⅓ to ½ cup granulated sugar
½ cup butter, cut into 8 pieces

¾ cup raisins
1¾ cups half-and-half
1 egg
1 teaspoon granulated sugar

1 Preheat oven to 375° F. Grease a cookie sheet.

2 In a large bowl, stir together flour, baking powder, salt, and sugar. Using two knives, cut in cold butter and blend until mixture is crumbly and the size of peas. Add raisins and toss. Slowly pour in half-and-half while mixing. Mix vigorously for five seconds.

3 Roll dough out on a lightly floured board to a thickness of ¾ inch. Cut with a 3-inch round cutter lightly dipped in flour. Place scones on prepared cookie sheet about 2 inches apart.

4 Make egg wash by beating egg and sugar together. Brush lightly on the top of each scone.

5 Bake for 25 to 30 minutes, or until slightly golden in color.

Yield: 14 large scones

Pumpkin Bread

Moist and spicy, this has the longest shelf life of any quick bread that I know of. It's heavenly spread with cream cheese and accompanied by hot tea.

2 cups granulated sugar
1 cup vegetable oil
4 eggs
2 cups mashed fresh pumpkin, *or* 1 (16 ounce) can solid-packed pumpkin (not pumpkin pie filling)
3 cups all-purpose flour

2 teaspoons baking soda
½ teaspoon salt
1 teaspoon ground cinnamon
1 teaspoon ground cloves
1 teaspoon ground nutmeg
½ teaspoon ground allspice
¾ cup water
1 cup chopped walnuts

1 Preheat oven to 350° F. Grease two 9- by 5- by 3-inch loaf pans.

2 In a large bowl, mix all ingredients except nuts with an electric mixer. Stir in chopped nuts. Pour batter evenly into prepared pans.

3 Bake for 1 hour, or until center springs back when lightly touched.

Yield: 2 loaves

Cranberry-Nut Bread

This makes a moist, sweet-tart holiday loaf, perfect for gift giving.

2 cups all-purpose flour
¾ cup granulated sugar
1½ teaspoons baking powder
1 teaspoon salt
½ teaspoon baking soda
3 tablespoons butter

¾ cup orange juice
1 egg, lightly beaten
1 tablespoon grated orange rind
1½ cups coarsely chopped
   cranberries
¾ cup chopped pecans

1 Preheat oven to 350° F. Grease a 9- by 5- by 3-inch loaf pan.

2 In a large bowl, stir together flour, sugar, baking powder, salt, and baking soda. Cut in butter with a pastry blender. Stir in orange juice, egg, and orange rind. Fold in cranberries and nuts. Spoon into prepared loaf pan.

3 Bake for 50 to 60 minutes, or until a cake tester inserted in center comes out clean.

Yield: 1 loaf

Buttermilk Biscuits

  Quick and easy! These buttery, flaky biscuits will add a nice touch to any meal with very little effort.

2 cups all-purpose flour
¾ teaspoon baking soda
2 teaspoons baking powder
1 teaspoon salt

1 tablespoon granulated sugar
6 tablespoons butter
1 cup buttermilk

1 Preheat oven to 400° F. Grease a cookie sheet.

2 In a large bowl, stir together flour, baking soda, baking powder, salt, and sugar. Add butter and mix with hands until crumbly. With a fork, slowly stir in buttermilk until all ingredients are just moistened.

3 Put dough on a lightly floured board and knead about 30 seconds. Roll out ½ inch thick and cut with a round cutter dipped in flour. Place biscuits 2 inches apart on cookie sheet.

4 Bake for 15 to 20 minutes, or until slightly golden.

Yield: 12 biscuits

Healthy Goodies

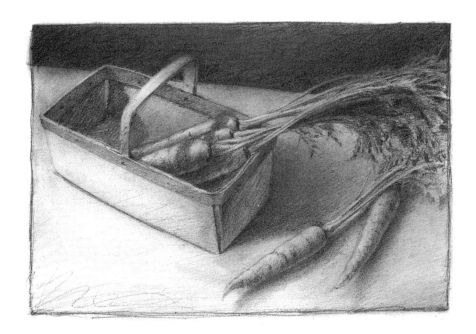

Low-Fat Cheesecake

Cindy Berglin, a pie baker at the bake shop, gave me this idea for a cheesecake. Plan to make this dessert twenty-four hours in advance.

Crust

1 cup graham-cracker crumbs

2 tablespoons margarine, melted

Filling

One 3-ounce box lemon Jell-O
1 cup boiling water
2 pounds nonfat plain yogurt
1 cup evaporated skim milk

1 pound part-skim ricotta cheese
⅓ cup granulated sugar
1 teaspoon vanilla extract

---

1 *To prepare crust*: Mix graham-cracker crumbs and margarine. Press mixture into the bottom of a 9-inch springform pan and refrigerate until ready to use.

2 *To prepare filling*: Put yogurt in a jelly bag, a cheesecloth bag, or a yogurt-cheese funnel in a 2-cup measuring cup; drain overnight in a cool place or in the refrigerator. Yogurt will become very thick.

3 In a small bowl, mix boiling water and Jell-O, stirring until dissolved, then chill until the consistency of egg whites.

4 Place evaporated skim milk in freezer for ½ hour.

5 With an electric mixer combine yogurt, ricotta cheese, sugar, and vanilla. Beat in Jell-O.

6 In a separate bowl, whip evaporated milk until thick and fold it into the yogurt mixture. Pour into prepared crust and refrigerate for several hours, or until firm.

Yield: one 9-inch cake

Oat-Bran Muffins

No new product has taken off as fast as these muffins.
They are moist and flavorful—you almost forget that
they are healthy for you because they taste so fantastic!

2 cups whole-wheat flour
2 cups oat bran
1 teaspoon baking powder
2 teaspoons baking soda
1 teaspoon salt
½ cup vegetable oil

4 egg whites
1 cup molasses
1½ cups low-fat or nonfat plain
   yogurt
1 cup raisins
½ cup unsweetened applesauce

1 Preheat oven to 400° F. Grease fifteen 3- by 1½-inch muffin cups.

2 In a large bowl, stir together flour, oat bran, baking powder, baking soda, and salt.

3 In another large bowl, combine oil, egg whites, and molasses. Add yogurt, raisins, and applesauce. Mix well.

4 Fold dry ingredients into wet ingredients. Spoon mixture evenly into prepared muffin cups.

5 Bake for 15 minutes, or until centers spring back when touched.

Yield: 15 muffins

Whole-Wheat Muffins

These muffins are wonderful served warm with
homemade apple butter!

2 cups whole-wheat flour
1 tablespoon baking powder
½ teaspoon salt
2 egg whites
¼ cup vegetable oil

1¼ cups skim milk
¼ cup honey
1 tablespoon grated orange rind
1 cup dried fruit: apricots, dates,
    raisins, etc.

1 Preheat oven to 400° F. Grease eleven 3- by 1½-inch muffin cups.

2 In a large bowl, combine flour, baking powder, and salt.

3 In a separate bowl, combine egg whites, oil, skim milk, honey, and orange rind. Add liquid ingredients to flour mixture. With a fork, mix just until dry ingredients are moistened. Fold in dried fruit. Spoon evenly into prepared muffin cups.

4 Bake for 18 to 20 minutes, or until a cake tester inserted in center of one muffin comes out clean. Remove pan to wire rack. Cool 5 minutes before removing muffins from pan; finish cooling on rack.

Yield: 11 muffins

Oat-Bran Apricot Bread

This makes a dense, hearty loaf with moist pieces of tart apricot.

1 cup dried apricots
2 cups whole-wheat flour
4 teaspoons baking powder
½ teaspoon baking soda
½ teaspoon salt
½ cup granulated sugar
2 tablespoons vegetable oil

2 egg whites
1 cup plain low-fat (or nonfat)
    yogurt
¼ cup skim milk
1 cup oat bran
1 cup chopped pecans
1 tablespoon grated orange rind

1 Preheat oven to 350° F. Grease a 9- by 5- by 3-inch loaf pan.

2 Boil apricots in 2 cups water until softened. Drain and cool.

3 In a large bowl, stir together flour, baking powder, baking soda, and salt.

4 In another large bowl, combine sugar and oil. Beat in egg whites, yogurt, and milk. Stir in oat bran, pecans, apricots, and grated orange rind. Add flour mixture and mix until well blended.

5 Spoon mixture into prepared pan. Pan will be very full, but don't worry because loaf doesn't rise too much.

6 Bake for 1 hour, or until center of loaf springs back when pressed with your finger. Remove pan to wire rack. Cool 10 minutes before removing bread from pan; finish cooling on rack.

Yield: 1 loaf

Oat-Bran Bread

*This is one of my favorite breads because I like to eat
things that taste great and that are also good for you.
My husband likes to cut this loaf in inch-thick slices for
toast. This bread keeps for several days.*

1 package dry yeast
½ cup warm water
3½ cups skim milk
⅔ cup molasses
2 tablespoons vegetable oil
1 tablespoon salt

3½ cups oat bran
2 cups whole-wheat flour
¼ cup wheat germ
¼ cup wheat bran
5½ cups all-purpose flour

1 In a large bowl, sprinkle yeast over the warm water. Stir until
dissolved and set aside for 5 minutes.

2 In a saucepan, heat skim milk and add molasses, oil, and salt. Cool
to lukewarm.

3 In a large bowl, stir together oat bran, whole-wheat flour, wheat
germ, wheat bran, and 3 cups of the all-purpose flour.

4 Add cooled milk mixture and oat bran–flour mixture to yeast
mixture. Beat for 5 minutes. Stir in the remaining 2½ cups of flour, turn
out onto a lightly floured board, and knead until smooth and elastic.

5 Transfer dough to a large oiled bowl, brush top with oil, cover bowl
with plastic wrap, and let rise until doubled in bulk.

6 Punch down the dough and divide into three equal portions. Form
dough into loaves and put the loaves into three greased 8½- by 4½- by
2½-inch loaf pans. Let loaves rise in a warm place until doubled in bulk.

7 Bake in a preheated oven at 350° F. for 35 to 45 minutes, or until loaves sound hollow when tapped with your finger.

Yield: 3 loaves

Pineapple-Macadamia Bread

This delicious bread is low in fat and high in fiber.

⅔ cup wheat bran
1 cup whole-wheat flour
2 teaspoons baking powder
¼ teaspoon baking soda
½ cup granulated sugar
1 teaspoon salt
2 egg whites

2 tablespoons vegetable oil
1 cup (16-ounce can) crushed
   pineapple, with syrup drained
   and reserved
1 cup macadamia chopped nuts (or
   substitute any other type of
   nut)

---

1 Preheat oven to 350° F. Grease a 9- by 5- by 3-inch loaf pan.

2 Place bran in a large bowl, pour 1 cup of reserved syrup over bran, and let soften.

3 In a medium-sized bowl, stir together flour, baking powder, baking soda, sugar, and salt; set aside.

4 Beat egg whites and oil into bran mixture. Stir in pineapple and nuts. Stir in flour mixture and mix well. Spoon batter into greased loaf pan.

5 Bake for 1 hour, or until center of loaf springs back when pressed with your finger. Remove bread from pan and cool on wire rack.

Yield: 1 loaf

Healthy Carrot Bread

Chock-full of carrots, walnuts, and raisins, this bread is low in fat.

1½ cups all-purpose flour
½ cup granulated sugar
1 teaspoon baking powder
1 teaspoon baking soda
½ teaspoon salt
1 teaspoon ground cinnamon
¼ teaspoon ground nutmeg

¼ teaspoon ground cloves
2 eggs
6 tablespoons vegetable oil
1 teaspoon vanilla extract
1¼ cups grated carrots
½ cup chopped walnuts
⅓ cup raisins

1 Preheat oven to 350° F. Grease a 9- by 5-inch loaf pan.

2 In a large bowl, stir together flour, sugar, baking powder, baking soda, salt, cinnamon, nutmeg, and cloves.

3 In another large bowl, beat eggs until well blended. Add oil, vanilla, and carrots. Beat until well mixed. Stir flour mixture into egg mixture until well blended. Fold in nuts and raisins. Spoon into prepared pan.

4 Bake for 45 minutes, or until a cake tester inserted in center comes out clean. Remove pan to wire rack. Cool 10 minutes before removing bread from pan; finish cooling on rack. Cool to room temperature. This loaf slices better if stored overnight.

Yield: 1 loaf

Strawberry Yogurt Pie

This pie is smooth, creamy, and light—great for a hot summer night!

Crust

1 cup graham-cracker crumbs
2 tablespoons light margarine,
  melted

1 teaspoon granulated sugar

Filling

1 package unflavored gelatin
½ cup orange juice
3 tablespoons granulated sugar
⅓ cup evaporated skim milk

1 tablespoon grated orange rind
½ teaspoon vanilla extract
1½ cups low-fat plain yogurt
2 cups thinly sliced fresh
  strawberries

1 *To prepare crust*: Combine graham-cracker crumbs, margarine, and sugar. Press firmly into a 9-inch pie pan. Press evenly up the sides and on the bottom. Refrigerate.

2 *To prepare filling*: Sprinkle gelatin over orange juice in a small saucepan. Add sugar and heat until gelatin is dissolved. Add evaporated skim milk, orange rind, and vanilla; stir well. Refrigerate until mixture is the consistency of egg whites.

3 Remove from refrigerator and beat with an electric mixer until light and fluffy. Add yogurt and whip again. Fold in strawberries and pour into prepared crust. Refrigerate until firm, about 3 hours.

Yield: one 9-inch pie

Cakes

Devil's Food Cake

*Before I went into business, I wanted to develop a
chocolate cake that was dense, moist, dark, and full of
flavor. I used to bake a cake every day until I got it
right. Well, ten pounds later, I came up with this
recipe, which has been successful for ten years!*

2¼ cups cake flour
2 teaspoons baking soda
½ teaspoon salt
1 cup butter, softened
2¼ cups firmly packed dark-brown
   sugar
3 eggs

3 squares (3 ounces) unsweetened
   chocolate, melted
½ cup buttermilk
1 cup boiling water
2 teaspoons vanilla extract
Mocha Icing (see page 74),
   Chocolate Icing (see page 75),
   or Cream-Cheese Icing (see
   page 81)

1 Preheat oven to 350° F. Grease and flour two 9-inch pans or three 8-inch round pans.

2 In a large bowl, sift together flour, baking soda, and salt.

3 In another large bowl, cream butter and sugar with an electric mixer. Add eggs one at a time, mixing well after each addition. Stir in melted chocolate.

4 Add flour mixture and buttermilk alternately to the butter mixture in three stages. Add boiling water and vanilla. Mix well, but don't overmix. Mixture will be very thin, so don't be alarmed. Pour batter into prepared pans.

5 Bake for 30 minutes, or until a cake tester inserted in center comes out clean. Remove pans to wire rack. Cool 5 to 10 minutes before removing cake from pans; finish cooling on rack.

6 Frost with icing of choice.

Yield: one 9-inch,
2-layer cake or
one 8-inch, 3-layer
cake

Mocha Icing

This icing is not too sweet yet is heavy on the coffee flavor. Just add less instant-coffee powder if you prefer a milder flavor.

3 cups heavy cream
1 cup confectioners' sugar
½ cup unsweetened cocoa powder

1½ tablespoons instant-coffee
  powder

1 In a large bowl, combine all ingredients and refrigerate, covered, for ½ hour.

2 Remove from refrigerator. Using an electric mixer, beat until stiff.

Yield: enough icing for
two 9-inch cake layers

Chocolate Icing

This makes a very smooth and creamy icing that's perfect on yellow cake.

½ cup butter
1½ cups semisweet chocolate chips
⅔ cup milk

1 teaspoon vanilla extract
1 cup confectioners' sugar

1 Melt butter and chocolate chips in the top of a double boiler. Stir in milk. Add vanilla. Stir in sugar.

2 Chill mixture for 45 minutes, then beat with an electric mixer every 15 minutes (chilling mixture between beatings) until it becomes light and thick enough to spread. (This will take three or four beatings.)

Yield: 3½ cups, or
enough to ice a 9-inch
layer cake

Yellow Cake

My grandmother's favorite cake is yellow cake with chocolate icing. It took me years to come up with a yellow cake that would pass both her and my Mom's test, but finally, on my grandmother's eighty-third birthday, I presented her with a cake we all enjoyed.

2½ cups all-purpose flour
½ teaspoon baking soda
1 teaspoon baking powder
1 teaspoon salt
1 cup butter, softened

2 cups granulated sugar
5 eggs, separated
1 teaspoon vanilla extract
1 cup sour cream
Icing of choice

1 Preheat oven to 350° F. Grease and flour two 9-inch round cake pans.

2 In a large bowl, sift together flour, baking soda, baking powder, and salt.

3 In another large bowl, cream butter and sugar with an electric mixer until light and fluffy. Add egg yolks one at a time, mixing well after each addition. Beat in vanilla. Add dry ingredients alternately with the sour cream, ending with the dry ingredients.

4 In a separate bowl, beat egg whites until stiff. Fold egg whites into cake batter, and pour into prepared pans.

5 Bake for 25 to 30 minutes, or until a cake tester inserted in center comes out clean. Remove pans to wire rack. Cool 10 minutes before removing cake from pans; finish cooling on rack.

6 Use your choice of icing; I like chocolate (see page 75) because it's so traditional and old-fashioned.

Yield: one 9-inch,
2-layer cake

White Layer Cake

This is an old family recipe from my friend Barbara Bruzdoski. I like this iced with whipped cream and covered with coconut—perfect as a spring dessert.

3 cups cake flour
2½ teaspoons baking powder
1 teaspoon salt
1 cup vegetable shortening
2 cups granulated sugar

2 teaspoons vanilla extract
1 cup milk
5 egg whites
1 recipe Coconut Icing (see page 79)

1 Preheat oven to 350° F. Grease and flour two 9-inch round cake pans.

2 In a large bowl, sift flour and measure 3 cups. Resift with baking powder and salt.

3 In another large bowl, cream shortening and sugar with an electric mixer. Add vanilla and mix well. Slowly add flour mixture to sugar mixture and mix well. Add milk and mix.

4 In another bowl, beat egg whites until stiff, and fold into cake mix. Pour batter evenly into prepared pans.

5 Bake for 30 minutes, or until a cake tester inserted in center comes out clean. Remove pans to wire rack. Cool 10 minutes before removing cake from pans; finish cooling on rack.

6 Split cakes to make four layers. Spread each layer with Coconut Icing cream mixture and top with coconut. Repeat until fourth layer is positioned. Ice sides and top of cake with remaining cream; cover entire cake with coconut. Refrigerate 1 hour before serving.

Yield: one 9-inch,
2-layer cake

Coconut Icing

A very light icing for angel food cake or any other favorite.

1 quart heavy cream
¼ cup confectioners' sugar

½ teaspoon almond extract
1 package (7 ounces) sweetened
    shredded coconut

1 Whip heavy cream with sugar and almond extract.

2 After icing cake with cream mixture, cover entire surface with coconut.

3 Refrigerate 1 hour before serving.

Yield: enough icing for
four 9-inch cake layers

Carrot Cake

This is our most popular cake; it seems that every year its sales double! It is very moist, keeps for at least a week in the refrigerator, and freezes perfectly.

2 cups all-purpose flour
2 teaspoons baking powder
1½ teaspoons baking soda
1 teaspoon salt
2 teaspoons ground cinnamon
1¾ cups granulated sugar

1½ cups vegetable oil
4 eggs
2 cups grated carrots
½ cup chopped walnuts
1 cup crushed and drained
  pineapple
1 recipe Cream-Cheese Icing (see
  page 81)

1 Preheat oven to 350° F. Grease and flour two 9-inch round cake pans.

2 In a large bowl, stir together flour, baking powder, baking soda, salt, and cinnamon.

3 In another large bowl, mix sugar and oil. Beat in eggs with an electric mixer. Stir in carrots, nuts, and pineapple. Stir in flour mixture. Pour into prepared pans.

4 Bake for 45 minutes, or until a cake tester inserted in center comes out clean. Remove pans to wire rack. Cool 15 minutes before removing cake from pans; finish cooling on rack.

5 Spread Cream-Cheese Icing between 9-inch layers and on sides and top of cake.

Yield: one 9-inch,
2-layer cake

Cream-Cheese Icing

This is my favorite icing—very creamy and not too sweet. It's delicious on chocolate cake as well as carrot cake.

1 pound cream cheese
½ cup butter, softened
2 teaspoons vanilla extract

2½ cups confectioners' sugar
3 tablespoons pineapple juice
 (optional)

In a large bowl, cream together cream cheese and butter with an electric mixer. Add vanilla and mix. Beat in sugar. Scrape down sides of bowl and beat again. Add pineapple juice, if desired, and mix well.

Yield: enough icing for
two 9-inch cake layers

Blueberry Buckle

My "Aunt" Norma used to bring this cake every time she came to visit us. Blueberries are my all-time favorite fruit, so what could be better than a moist cake full of berries and topped with a sugary, cinnamon crumb?

½ cup butter
¾ cup granulated sugar
1 egg
½ cup milk

2 teaspoons baking powder
½ teaspoon salt
2 cups all-purpose flour
2½ cups blueberries

Topping

1 cup firmly packed dark-brown sugar
⅔ cup all-purpose flour

1 teaspoon ground cinnamon
½ cup butter

---

1 Preheat oven to 375° F. Grease a 9-inch square pan.

2 In a large bowl, cream butter and sugar. Add egg, milk, baking powder, and salt. Mix well. Stir in flour 1 cup at a time. Fold in blueberries. Pour batter into prepared pan and set aside.

3 *To make topping*: Combine all ingredients in a medium-sized bowl. Mix with a pastry cutter or your hands until combined and crumbly. Sprinkle evenly on top of cake batter.

4 Bake for 45 to 50 minutes, or until a cake tester inserted in center comes out clean.

Yield: one 9-inch
square buckle

Crumb Cake

 This cake is quick and easy to make. Serve it warm for an extra-special breakfast or morning coffee.

4 tablespoons butter
¾ cup granulated sugar
1 egg
¾ cup milk

1½ cups all-purpose flour
2½ teaspoons baking powder
¾ teaspoon salt

Crumb Topping

⅔ cup firmly packed dark-brown
    sugar
½ cup all-purpose flour

1 teaspoon ground cinnamon
6 tablespoons chilled butter

---

1 Preheat oven to 375° F. Grease a 9-inch square pan.

2 In a large bowl, blend butter, sugar, egg, milk, flour, baking powder, and salt. Beat vigorously for 30 seconds. Spread into prepared pan and set aside.

3 *To make crumb topping:* In a small bowl, combine brown sugar, flour, cinnamon, and butter. Mix with a pastry cutter or your fingers until combined and crumbly. Sprinkle evenly on top of cake batter.

4 Bake for 25 to 30 minutes, or until a cake tester inserted in center comes out clean. Cut into squares and serve warm.

Yield: one 9-inch
square cake

Apricot Coffee Cake

This is a rich sour-cream cake studded with tart apricots and swirled with brown sugar and cinnamon.

Streusel Mixture

1 cup firmly packed dark-brown
   sugar
4 tablespoons butter, softened

¼ cup all-purpose flour
2 teaspoons ground cinnamon

Coffee Cake

2 cups dried apricots
3 cups all-purpose flour
1½ teaspoons baking powder
¾ teaspoon baking soda
¼ teaspoon salt
¾ cup butter, softened

1¼ cups granulated sugar
4 eggs
1½ teaspoons vanilla extract
1 cup sour cream
Confectioners' sugar

---

1 Preheat oven to 350° F. Grease and flour a 10-inch tube pan.

2 *To make streusel mixture:* Combine all streusel ingredients and mix with a fork or hands until crumbly; set aside.

3 Chop apricots.

4 In a large bowl, sift together flour, baking powder, baking soda, and salt.

5 Put butter in a large bowl and beat until fluffy with an electric mixer. Gradually beat in sugar. Add eggs one at a time. Beat for 3 minutes. Add vanilla.

6 Add flour mixture to butter mixture alternately in three stages with the sour cream. Fold in apricots. Spoon one-third of the mixture into prepared pan. Sprinkle one-half of Streusel Mixture onto cake batter. Spoon one-third more cake batter on top of streusel. Sprinkle on rest of Streusel Mixture and spoon rest of cake mixture on top.

7 Bake for 55 to 60 minutes, or until a cake tester inserted in center comes out clean. Remove pan to wire rack. When cake is cool, remove from pan onto platter. Sprinkle with confectioners' sugar.

Yield: one 10-inch
tube cake

Whiskey Cake

When I was in high school, I used to work as a receptionist at South Fork Appliance, which was owned by Hank Szczepanik. This was his family's favorite cake, and I used to make it for them on holidays and for birthdays. It's not too sweet and not as strong-tasting as a rum cake.

3 cups all-purpose flour
½ teaspoon baking powder
¾ teaspoon baking soda
¼ teaspoon salt
¾ cup butter, softened
1 cup granulated sugar

4 eggs
1½ teaspoons vanilla extract
½ cup buttermilk
½ cup whiskey
1 cup chopped walnuts

Glaze

½ cup butter
¼ cup water

1 cup granulated sugar
½ cup whiskey

---

1 Preheat oven to 350° F. Grease and flour a 10-inch Bundt pan.

2 In a large bowl, sift together flour, baking powder, baking soda, and salt.

3 In another large bowl, beat butter with an electric mixer until fluffy. Gradually beat in sugar. Add eggs one at a time. Beat for 3 minutes. Add vanilla.

4 Add dry ingredients to butter mixture alternately in three stages with buttermilk and whiskey. Pour into prepared pan.

5 Bake for 5 minutes. Sprinkle top with 1 cup chopped walnuts and bake for 40 minutes more, or until a cake tester inserted in center comes out clean. Remove pan to wire rack. Cool cake in pan.

6 *To make glaze*: In a medium-sized saucepan, combine first three ingredients and boil for 5 minutes. Stir in whiskey.

7 Remove cooled cake to a serving platter and slowly dribble glaze over cake in stages until all the glaze has been soaked up by the cake.

Yield: one 10-inch
Bundt cake

Date-Banana Cake

A professor of mine, Bob Sielaff, gave me this recipe, which he received from his friend Patty Feurst. This was her grandmother's favorite cake, and the students have been serving it at many affairs at Cobleskill College.

1½ cups boiling water
1½ cups old-fashioned rolled oats
1½ cups all-purpose flour
½ teaspoon ground cinnamon
¾ teaspoon ground cloves
¾ teaspoon baking powder
½ teaspoon baking soda
¾ teaspoon salt
¾ cup butter
¾ cup granulated sugar

3 eggs
1½ cups firmly packed dark-brown
　sugar
¾ cup fully ripe mashed banana
¾ cup chopped dates
¾ cup chopped walnuts
3 cups whipped cream or 1 recipe
　Cream-Cheese Icing (see page
　81)

1　Preheat oven to 350° F. Grease and flour two 9-inch layer pans.

2　In a medium-sized bowl, pour boiling water over oats and let stand.

3　In a large bowl, sift together flour, cinnamon, cloves, baking powder, baking soda, and salt.

4　In another large bowl, cream butter and granulated sugar with an electric mixer. Beat in eggs until smooth. Add oat mixture.

5　Stir dry ingredients into butter mixture. Stir in brown sugar. When mixture is thoroughly blended, add bananas, dates, and walnuts. Pour mixture evenly into prepared pans.

6 Bake for 50 minutes, or until firm. Remove pans to wire rack. Cool for 15 minutes before removing cake from pans; finish cooling on rack.

7 Frost with whipped cream or Cream-Cheese Icing.

Yield: one 9-inch,
2-layer cake

Applesauce Cake

This recipe came to me through the mail in an attempt to get me involved in a recipe exchange letter. I never got involved in the letter, but I did try the cake. It's a heavy, wholesome cake that lasts a long time. It's prettier with the glaze, but just as nice without it.

¾ cup butter, softened
2 cups granulated sugar
2 eggs
2 cups unsweetened applesauce
2 teaspoons baking soda
3 cups all-purpose flour
½ teaspoon salt

1½ teaspoons ground nutmeg
1 teaspoon baking powder
1 teaspoon ground cloves
1 tablespoon ground cinnamon
1 cup raisins
1 cup chopped walnuts

Glaze

2 cups confectioners' sugar

3 to 4 tablespoons apple juice or lemon juice

1 Preheat oven to 300° F. Grease and flour a 10-inch Bundt pan.

2 In a large bowl, cream butter, sugar, and eggs with an electric mixer.

3 In a separate bowl combine applesauce and baking soda and set aside.

4 In a large bowl, stir together flour, salt, nutmeg, baking powder, cloves, and cinnamon. Add flour mixture to butter mixture and beat again. Stir in applesauce mixture, raisins, and walnuts. Pour into prepared pan.

5 Bake for 1 hour 10 minutes, or until a cake tester inserted in center comes out clean. Remove pan to wire rack. Cool 10 minutes before removing cake from pan; finish cooling on rack.

6 *To make glaze:* Combine sugar and juice and mix well.

7 When cake is cool, drizzle glaze with a spoon so that it drips down sides and covers top of cake.

Yield: one 10-inch
Bundt cake

Chocolate Mousse Cake

At a cake party for my friend Betsy's birthday, this cake won rave reviews. It's an elegant dessert that can be made a day in advance with very little effort.

3 cups chocolate wafer crumbs
9 tablespoons butter, melted
2¾ cups semisweet chocolate chips

2 eggs
4 eggs, separated
2 cups heavy cream

Topping

1½ cups heavy cream
2 tablespoons granulated sugar

1 teaspoon vanilla extract

---

1 Grind chocolate wafers in a blender. Place them in a small bowl and add melted butter. Press crumb mixture into a 10-inch springform pan, covering the bottom and sides evenly. Refrigerate.

2 In the top of a double boiler, melt chocolate chips. Remove from heat and transfer softened chocolate to a large bowl. Add whole eggs and mix well, using an electric mixer. Add egg yolks and mix. Scrape down sides of bowl and mix again.

3 In a separate bowl, whip heavy cream until soft peaks form.

4 In another bowl, beat egg whites until stiff. Fold cream and egg whites into chocolate mixture until completely incorporated. Pour mixture into prepared crust and chill overnight.

5 *To make topping:* Whip 1½ cups heavy cream with sugar and vanilla.

6 Cover cake evenly with cream topping 1 hour before serving. Loosen crust on all sides using a sharp knife and remove sides of springform pan.

Yield: one 10-inch
round cake

Chocolate-Chip Cheesecake

Our daytime manager, Nancy Boden, gave me this recipe. She has been making it for years, and it has become a family favorite.

Crust

1 cup graham-cracker crumbs
¼ cup confectioners' sugar

4 tablespoons butter, melted

Filling

5 packages (8 ounces each) cream cheese
1¼ cups granulated sugar
3 tablespoons all-purpose flour
1 teaspoon vanilla extract

5 eggs
2 egg yolks
½ cup Bailey's Irish Cream liqueur
1 cup semisweet chocolate chips, chopped

---

1 Preheat oven to 450° F.

2 *To prepare crust:* Combine graham-cracker crumbs, sugar, and melted butter. Press mixture into bottom of a 9- or 10-inch springform pan. Refrigerate.

3 *To prepare filling:* In a large bowl, beat cream cheese with an electric mixer. Add sugar, flour, and vanilla. Mix well. Scrape down sides of bowl and mix again. Add eggs and egg yolks one at a time, mixing and scraping down sides of bowl after each addition. Stir in Irish Cream and chocolate chips. Pour into crust.

4 Bake for 15 minutes. Reduce temperature to 250° F. and bake for 1 hour longer, or until firm. Remove pan to wire rack. Cool completely before removing cake from pan. Refrigerate at least 4 hours, or overnight.

Yield: one 10-inch cake

Pineapple
Upside-Down Cake

*This impressive-looking cake is delicious served warm
with whipped cream.*

Three 8¼-ounce cans sliced
    pineapple rings in heavy syrup
4 tablespoons butter
½ cup firmly packed light-brown
    sugar
⅓ cup pecan halves
1 cup all-purpose flour

½ cup granulated sugar
1½ teaspoons baking powder
½ teaspoon salt
5 tablespoons butter
½ cup milk
1 egg

1 Preheat oven to 350° F.

2 Drain pineapple slices, reserving 2 tablespoons of the syrup.

3 In a 10-inch iron skillet with a heat-resistant handle, melt butter
over medium heat. Add brown sugar, stirring until sugar is melted.
Remove from heat.

4 Arrange eight pineapple slices around edge of pan on sugar mixture,
overlapping slices slightly. Put one slice in center of skillet. Fill
pineapple centers with pecan halves. Halve three pineapple slices and
arrange around sides of skillet, curved-side down. Put pecans in center.

5 In a medium-sized bowl, sift together flour, sugar, baking powder,
and salt. Add the 5 tablespoons of butter and milk and beat with an
electric mixer on high speed for 2 minutes. Add egg and 2 tablespoons
reserved pineapple syrup. Beat 2 minutes more. Pour cake batter over
pineapple in skillet, spreading evenly.

6 Bake for 40 to 45 minutes, or until cake springs back when lightly pressed with fingertip. Remove skillet to wire rack and cool for 5 minutes. Place serving platter over cake and turn pan upside down. Lift off skillet.

Yield: one 10-inch cake

Angel Food Cake

*Fluffy and light, this cake is great for dieters because it
contains no fat. If you are not watching calories, serve
it with fresh whipped cream and berries or cut it up
and use it with chocolate fondue.*

1¼ cups cake flour
1½ cups granulated sugar
1¾ cups egg whites, at room
   temperature
½ teaspoon salt

1½ teaspoons cream of tartar
1 teaspoon vanilla extract
½ teaspoon almond extract

1 Preheat oven to 375° F.

2 Sift flour with ¼ cup of the sugar. Resift three times.

3 In another large bowl, combine egg whites, salt, and cream of tartar.
Beat at medium speed with an electric mixer until soft peaks form when
beater is raised. At high speed, gradually add remaining ¼ cup sugar, ¼
cup at a time. Continue beating until stiff peaks form when beater is
raised. Fold in vanilla and almond extracts.

4 Fold one-quarter of the flour mixture into the egg whites. Continue
folding in flour mixture in three more stages. Gently push batter into
ungreased 10-inch tube pan. With a knife, cut through batter to remove
any large air bubbles. Place pan on lowest rack in oven.

5 Bake for 30 minutes, or until cake springs back when lightly pressed
with fingertip. Invert pan over the neck of a bottle to cool completely.
When cool, loosen cake from sides of pan with a knife and turn out
onto cake platter.

Yield: one 10-inch cake

Dee's Refrigerator Cheesecake

When I was written up in Family Circle *magazine, Dee Steinbach wrote to me from Chicago, asking to come out and visit. She wanted to open her own bake shop and was interested in a few tips. She was a lot of fun and we had a great time during her stay. When she got home, she sent me this recipe, which is unlike most cheesecakes I know—light and refreshing and great for summer!*

Crust

1 cup graham-cracker crumbs
¼ cup confectioners' sugar

4 tablespoons butter, melted

Filling

One 3-ounce package lemon Jell-O
1 cup boiling water
2 packages (8 ounces each) cream
  cheese

½ cup granulated sugar
1 teaspoon vanilla extract
1 cup heavy cream

---

1 Dissolve Jell-O in boiling water. Chill until slightly thickened (about the consistency of egg whites).

2 *To prepare crust:* Combine graham-cracker crumbs, confectioners' sugar, and butter in a small bowl. Press into bottom of a 9-inch springform pan. Refrigerate.

3 *To prepare filling:* In a large bowl, beat cream cheese, sugar, and vanilla until fluffy, using an electric mixer. Beat in Jell-O mixture.

4 In a separate bowl, beat cream until thick; fold it into cream-cheese mixture. Pour into prepared crust and refrigerate for several hours.

Yield: one 9-inch cake

Cheesecake

This is another great recipe that my friend "Grandma" Esposito gave me when I was looking for a heavy, thick cheesecake. This cake is a favorite of many, including one special friend for whom I make it every year as a birthday cake.

1 recipe Graham Cracker Crust
   (see page 105)
4 packages (8 ounces each) cream
   cheese

2 cups granulated sugar
8 eggs, separated
2 cups sour cream
2 tablespoons vanilla extract

1 Prepare Graham Cracker Crust. Press evenly into bottom of a 10-inch springform pan. Refrigerate.

2 Preheat oven to 350° F.

3 To prepare filling, in a large bowl, and using an electric mixer, cream the cheese. Add sugar and mix well. Add egg yolks one at a time. Scrape down bowl and mix again. Mix in sour cream and vanilla.

4 In a separate bowl, beat egg whites until stiff. Fold egg whites into cream-cheese mixture. Pour into crust. (For best results, place pan in a roasting pan half-filled with boiling water.)

5 Bake for 1 hour and 20 minutes, or until cake is golden brown and firm. Cool in the oven with the door half open for 1 hour, then remove and refrigerate overnight.

Yield: one 10-inch cake

Pound Cake

I made pound cake five times before I got the right flavor and texture. This is dense, moist, and buttery. It's on the plain side, but it's a favorite of many people who don't like heavy, gooey desserts.

3 cups all-purpose flour
¼ teaspoon salt
1½ cups butter, softened
2½ cups granulated sugar

8 eggs, separated
2 teaspoons vanilla extract
Grated rind of 1 lemon and 1
    orange

1 Preheat oven to 350° F. Grease and flour a 10-inch tube pan.

2 In a large bowl, sift together flour and salt.

3 In another large bowl, cream butter and sugar with an electric mixer until light and fluffy. Add egg yolks one at a time. Add vanilla and rind; mix well. Add 1 cup of flour mixture at a time to butter mixture. Scrape down sides and mix well.

4 In another bowl, beat egg whites until stiff. With an electric mixer on low speed, fold in egg whites until thoroughly combined. Spoon mixture into prepared pan.

5 Bake for 1 hour and 10 minutes, or until center of cake springs back when pressed with your finger. Remove pan to wire rack. Cool 15 minutes before removing cake from pan; finish cooling on rack.

6 Leave plain, dust with confectioners' sugar, or ice with your favorite icing.

Yield: one 10-inch
tube cake

No-Citron Fruit Cake

One Christmas, my friend Barbara Bruzdoski brought my family this fruit cake. We all dislike citron, and to our pleasant surprise this cake didn't contain any at all. It has a very festive appeal and it lasts one month in the refrigerator, which is an added bonus during the Christmas rush.

1 pound dried fruit: pears, apricots, peaches, pineapples, etc.
12 ounces dried pitted prunes
10 ounces dried pitted dates
4 ounces dried figs
½ cup cream sherry
1½ cups all-purpose flour
¾ cup granulated sugar
1 teaspoon baking powder
Two 12-ounce cans salted mixed nuts (no peanuts)
1½ cups pecans
6 eggs, lightly beaten

1 Preheat oven to 300° F. Line a 10-inch tube pan with foil, pressing out wrinkles so cake surface will be smooth.

2 In a large bowl or pot, combine dried fruits and sherry and let stand for 15 minutes, stirring occasionally.

3 In another large bowl, stir together flour, sugar, and baking powder.

4 Stir mixed nuts and pecans into fruit mixture. Remove 1½ cups and set aside.

5 Stir flour mixture into fruit-and-nut mixture, making sure everything is well coated. Stir in eggs and mix well. Spoon batter into prepared pan. Pack firmly to eliminate air pockets. Sprinkle reserved 1½ cups fruit-and-nut mixture on top.

6 Cover pan loosely with aluminum foil and bake for 2 hours. Remove foil and bake for another ½ hour, or until cake tester inserted in center comes out clean. Remove pan to wire rack. Cool cake for 30 minutes before peeling off foil and removing cake from pan. Finish cooling on rack.

7 Wrap fruit cake tightly with foil or plastic wrap. Store in refrigerator or any cool place.

Yield: one 10-inch cake

Fruit Pies
and Cream Pies

Pie Pastry

This is a good, all-purpose crust for a double-crust pie. It's quite flaky and buttery and can be halved for a single-crust pie.

1¼ cups all-purpose flour
¼ teaspoon salt
½ cup butter

3 tablespoons cold water
1 tablespoon fresh lemon juice

1 In a medium-sized bowl combine flour and salt. Cut in butter with a pastry blender, two knives, or with your hands. When mixture is the size of peas, add water and lemon juice. Toss gently with a fork.

2 Divide pastry into two equal halves. Roll out one half on a lightly floured surface, in a circle 3 inches larger than the pie pan you plan on using. Fit round into pie pan and either flute edges by turning excess underneath around the edge of the rim, or leave as is for a double-crust pie.

3 For a top crust, roll out second half the same size and shape and place over filling. Seal edges; trim and flute as desired.

Yield: enough pastry for
a double-crust pie

Graham-Cracker Crust

This makes a perfect crust for Cheesecake.

1 cup graham-cracker crumbs   4 tablespoons butter, melted
2 tablespoons confectioners' sugar

1 In a small bowl, combine all ingredients until well mixed.

2 Place mixture in a 9-inch pie pan and press crumbs evenly against the bottom and sides of the pan. Refrigerate.

Yield: one 9-inch crust
or bottom crust of a 9-
or 10-inch springform
pan

Apple Pie

One of my fondest memories is of sitting with my best friend Betsy on a cold, snowy night about twelve years ago. Everything was so quiet, and we sat for hours chatting and eating warm apple pie with vanilla ice cream. Now, every time it snows I think about warming up this homey pie.

1 unbaked 9-inch pie shell with top crust (see Pie Pastry, page 104)
½ cup granulated sugar
2 tablespoons all-purpose flour
¼ teaspoon ground nutmeg

¾ teaspoon ground cinnamon
6 cups peeled, cored, and sliced Granny Smith apples
1 tablespoon fresh lemon juice
2 tablespoons butter

1 Preheat oven to 400° F.

2 If making shell from scratch, use one recipe Pie Pastry. Arrange bottom crust in pan; set aside top crust.

3 In a small bowl combine sugar, flour, nutmeg, and cinnamon. Add spice mixture to apples and toss. Spoon apples into prepared pastry. Sprinkle with fresh lemon juice and dot with butter.

4 Cover apples with top crust, seal edges, trim, and flute as desired. Make six vents in top with a knife.

5 Bake for 1 hour, or until crust is golden. Remove pan to wire rack and cool for several minutes. Serve warm.

Yield: one 9-inch pie

Pumpkin Pie

This is our biggest seller at Thanksgiving. It's smooth and creamy with just the right amount of spice.

1 unbaked 10-inch pie shell (see
    Pie Pastry, page 104)
1 egg white, lightly beaten
2 eggs
⅔ cup milk
1⅓ cups evaporated milk
1 cup granulated sugar
1 tablespoon ground cinnamon

1 teaspoon ground ginger
⅛ teaspoon ground cloves
⅛ teaspoon ground nutmeg
½ teaspoon salt
1 pound (2 cups) mashed fresh or
    solid-packed pumpkin (not
    pumpkin-pie filling)

1 Preheat oven to 350° F.

2 If making shell from scratch, use one-half recipe Pie Pastry. Brush bottom with egg white and set aside.

3 In a large bowl, beat eggs. Add milk and evaporated milk and mix. Add sugar, cinnamon, ginger, cloves, nutmeg, and salt. Mix well. Add pumpkin and mix again. Pour mixture into prepared pie shell.

4 Bake for 1 hour, or until filling feels firm when lightly pressed with fingertip. Remove pan to wire rack and cool. Serve with whipped cream if desired.

Yield: one 10-inch pie

Toasted-Coconut–
Cream Pie

When my friend Wanda found out I was serving this creamy, rich pie for dessert, she found her way to our dinner table!

1 prebaked 9-inch pie shell (see Pie Pastry, page 104)
2 cups sweetened coconut
⅓ cup all-purpose flour
¼ teaspoon salt
¼ cup granulated sugar

½ cup milk
1½ cups hot milk
4 egg yolks
1 tablespoon butter
1 teaspoon vanilla extract

Topping

1 cup heavy cream
1 teaspoon vanilla extract

1 tablespoon granulated sugar (optional)

---

1 Preheat oven to 400° F.

2 If making shell from scratch, use one-half recipe Pie Pastry.

3 Prick crust with a fork to vent. Place a piece of waxed paper on crust and cover with rice. Bake for 20 minutes, or until golden. Remove pan to wire rack to cool. Lower oven temperature to 350° F.

4 Spread coconut on a cookie sheet and toast in oven for 10 minutes, tossing every few minutes. When golden brown, remove from oven and set aside.

5 In the top of a double boiler over boiling water, mix flour, salt, and sugar. Add ½ cup milk and stir until smooth. Add 1½ cups hot milk, stirring constantly, until the sauce is thick and smooth.

6 Beat egg yolks in a separate bowl; add ½ cup of sauce to the egg yolks, stirring constantly. Return mixture to the double boiler, stirring constantly. Cook for 3 minutes longer. Remove from heat; stir in butter and vanilla. Stir in 1½ cups of the toasted coconut. Pour mixture into cooled pie crust. Refrigerate.

7 *To prepare topping:* About 1 hour before serving, beat heavy cream, vanilla, and sugar until stiff. Pile cream on top of pie filling. Spread to edges of pie shell.

8 Sprinkle top with remaining coconut. Refrigerate. Pie can be made the night before, but top with cream the day it will be served.

Yield: one 9-inch pie

Cherry Crumb Pie

This pie is my brother's favorite and was a big success when I served it last Thanksgiving. The oatmeal-and-almond crumb stays nice and crunchy and is offset by the smooth, tart cherries.

1 unbaked 10-inch pie shell (see
  Pie Pastry, page 104)
1 cup cold water
¼ cup cornstarch
¾ cup granulated sugar

¼ teaspoon salt
5 cups fresh or frozen tart red
  cherries
1 tablespoon fresh lemon juice

Crumb Topping

⅓ cup quick-cooking rolled oats
⅓ cup firmly packed dark-brown
  sugar
½ cup butter, chilled

½ cup all-purpose flour
½ cup sliced almonds

1 Preheat oven to 375° F.

2 If making shell from scratch, use one-half recipe Pie Pastry. Set shell aside.

3 In a saucepan, combine water, cornstarch, sugar, and salt. Stir constantly over a low flame; when mixture begins to thicken, add cherries. Cook until mixture is clear red and begins to bubble. Stir in lemon juice. Pour into unbaked pie shell.

4 *To prepare crumb topping:* Combine all ingredients in a bowl. Mix with hands until well combined and crumbly.

5 Sprinkle crumb evenly on top of cherries.

6 Bake for 1 hour, or until topping is golden. Remove pan to wire rack and cool.

Yield: one 10-inch pie

Raspberry Pie

This pie is a beautiful red color, with a hint of orange.

1 unbaked 9-inch pie shell with
   top crust (see Pie Pastry, page
   104)
¾ cup granulated sugar
4 tablespoons all-purpose flour
Grated rind of 1 orange

6 cups raspberries
1 tablespoon fresh lemon juice
2 tablespoons butter

1 Preheat oven to 400° F.

2 If making shell from scratch, use one recipe Pie Pastry. Set shell aside.

3 In a large bowl, combine sugar, flour, and orange rind. Stir in raspberries and spoon mixture into prepared pastry bottom. Sprinkle lemon juice over fruit. Dot with butter. Cover mixture with top crust, seal edges, trim, and flute as desired. Make six vents in top with a knife.

4 Bake for 1 hour, or until crust is golden. Remove pan to wire rack to cool.

Yield: one 9-inch pie

Peach Crumb Pie

This is a wonderful way to use up ripe, bruised peaches.

1 unbaked 9-inch pie shell (see Pie
    Pastry, page 104)
1 egg white, lightly beaten
¼ cup firmly packed dark-brown
    sugar
½ teaspoon ground cinnamon

¼ teaspoon ground nutmeg
Dash of salt
5 tablespoons all-purpose flour
5 cups peeled and sliced peaches
1 tablespoon fresh lemon juice

Crumb Topping

¾ cup all-purpose flour
½ cup firmly packed dark-brown
    sugar

½ cup chopped almonds
6 tablespoons butter, chilled

1 Preheat oven to 375° F.

2 If making shell from scratch, use one-half recipe Pie Pastry. Brush bottom with egg white and set aside.

3 In a large bowl, stir together sugar, cinnamon, nutmeg, salt, and flour. Add prepared peaches and toss. Spoon mixture into prepared pie shell. Sprinkle lemon juice over peach mixture.

4 *To prepare crumb topping:* In a medium-sized bowl, stir together flour, sugar, almonds, and butter. Mix all ingredients until crumbly.

5 Sprinkle crumb evenly on top of peaches.

6 Bake for 1 hour, or until topping is golden. Remove pan to wire rack to cool.

Yield: one 9-inch pie

Pear Crumb Pie

This is a nice change from the traditional apple pie, and pears are a good fresh fruit to use in the winter when the choices are minimal. My husband turned his nose up at this the first time I baked it; he later ended up eating more than half the pie!

1 unbaked 9-inch pie shell (see Pie Pastry, page 104)
1 egg white, lightly beaten
¼ cup firmly packed dark-brown sugar
¼ cup minced, crystallized ginger

2 tablespoons fresh lemon juice
¼ teaspoon ground nutmeg
4 tablespoons all-purpose flour
5 cups peeled, cored, and sliced pears

Crumb Topping

⅓ cup all-purpose flour
¼ cup granulated sugar

¾ cup ground walnuts
6 tablespoons butter, chilled

1 Preheat oven to 375° F.

2 If making shell from scratch, use one-half recipe Pie Pastry. Brush bottom with egg white and set aside.

3 In a large bowl, combine brown sugar, ginger, lemon juice, nutmeg, and flour. Add pears and toss gently. Spoon pear mixture into prepared pie shell and set aside.

4 *To prepare crumb topping:* In a small bowl, combine flour, sugar, walnuts, and butter. Mix until crumbly.

5 Top pie with crumb mixture and spread evenly.

6 Bake for 1 hour, or until crust is golden and fruit is bubbly. If pie crust starts to get too brown before fruit is bubbly, cover with aluminum foil. Remove pan to wire rack to cool.

Yield: one 9-inch pie

Apple Crumb Pie

This pie is our biggest seller. If you like your apple pie on the sweeter side, this one's for you. The tart apples and the sweet crumb are an excellent combination.

1 unbaked 9-inch pie shell (see Pie Pastry, page 104)
⅓ cup granulated sugar
2 tablespoons all-purpose flour
¼ teaspoon ground nutmeg

¾ teaspoon ground cinnamon
5 cups peeled and sliced Granny Smith apples
1 tablespoon lemon juice

Crumb Topping

½ cup all-purpose flour
⅓ cup granulated sugar

4 tablespoons butter, chilled

1 Preheat oven to 375° F.

2 If making shell from scratch, use one-half recipe Pie Pastry. Set shell aside.

3 In a small bowl, combine sugar, flour, nutmeg, and cinnamon. Add spice mixture to apples and toss. Spoon apples into prepared pastry. Sprinkle with fresh lemon juice and set aside.

4 *To prepare crumb topping:* In a small bowl, combine flour, sugar, and butter. Using a pastry blender, mix until crumbly.

5 Sprinkle crumb evenly over apples.

6 Bake for 1 hour, or until topping is golden. Remove pan to wire rack to cool. Serve with vanilla ice cream, if desired.

Yield: one 9-inch pie

Blueberry Pie

*Nothing is better than homemade blueberry pie with
fresh cream or vanilla ice cream.*

1 unbaked 9-inch pie shell with
    top crust (see Pie Pastry, page
    104)
1 egg white, lightly beaten
½ cup granulated sugar
5 tablespoons all-purpose flour *or* 2
    tablespoons plus 1 teaspoon
    tapioca

5 cups blueberries
1 tablespoon fresh lemon juice
2 tablespoons butter

1 Preheat oven to 375° F.

2 If making shell and top from scratch, use one recipe Pie Pastry.
Arrange bottom crust in pan; set aside top crust. Brush bottom with egg
white and set aside.

3 In a large bowl, stir together sugar, flour or tapioca, and blueberries.
Toss mixture lightly and spoon into prepared pastry. Sprinkle lemon
juice over blueberry mixture. Dot top with butter.

4 Cover mixture with top crust, seal edges, trim, and flute as desired.
Make six vents in top with a knife.

5 Bake for 1 hour, or until crust is golden. Remove pan to wire rack
and cool completely before serving; if served hot it will be too runny.

Yield: one 9-inch pie

Strawberry-Rhubarb Pie

This pie has a lovely combination of sweet and tart, with a hint of orange. Even people who don't like rhubarb love this pie.

1 unbaked 9-inch pie shell and top crust (see Pie Pastry, page 104)
1 egg white, slightly beaten
⅓ cup all-purpose flour
1 cup granulated sugar
¼ cup orange juice

Grated rind of 1 orange
3 cups cleaned and hulled strawberries
3 cups sliced rhubarb (cut into 1-inch lengths)
1 tablespoon butter

1 Preheat oven to 400° F.

2 If making shell and top from scratch, use one recipe Pie Pastry. Arrange bottom crust in pan; set aside top crust. Brush bottom crust with egg white and set aside.

3 In a large bowl, stir together flour, sugar, orange juice, and orange rind. Mix well. Fold in the strawberries and rhubarb. Spoon mixture into prepared pie shell and dot the top with butter.

4 Cover mixture with top crust, seal edges, trim, and flute as desired. Cut a few slits in top crust to vent.

5 Bake for 1 hour, or until crust is golden. If edges brown too quickly, cover them with aluminum foil. Remove pan to wire rack and cool completely before slicing. Serve at room temperature.

Yield: one 9-inch pie

Pecan Pie

This pie is very rich and sweet. It's a great winter dessert.

1 unbaked 9-inch pie shell (see Pie Pastry, page 104)
3 eggs
½ cup firmly packed dark-brown sugar
1 cup corn syrup

½ cup butter, melted
½ teaspoon vanilla extract
1 cup pecan halves

1 Preheat oven to 350° F.

2 If making shell from scratch, use one-half recipe Pie Pastry. Set shell aside.

3 In a medium-sized bowl, beat eggs. Add brown sugar and mix well. Pour in corn syrup and mix. Add melted butter and vanilla. Mix well.

4 Arrange pecans in pie shell. Pour mixture into pie shell over pecans. Pecans will float to the top.

5 Bake for 45 minutes, or until pie is firm when jiggled. Remove pan to wire rack to cool.

Yield: one 9-inch pie

Banana Cream Pie

*This pie is smooth and creamy, with a lot of natural
sweetness from the ripe banana.*

One 9-inch graham-cracker crust
⅓ cup granulated sugar
½ cup all-purpose flour
½ teaspoon salt
2 cups half-and-half

3 egg yolks
2 tablespoons butter
1 teaspoon vanilla extract
2 large ripe bananas

Topping

1 cup heavy cream
1 teaspoon vanilla extract

---

1 Prepare crust (see page 105) and set aside.

2 In a medium-sized bowl, mix egg yolks slightly.

3 *Make custard:* In the top of a double boiler over boiling water,
combine sugar, flour, salt, and half-and-half. Stir constantly until
mixture begins to thicken and bubble. Add ½ cup hot mixture to egg
yolks and beat. Return egg-yolk mixture to double boiler and stir
constantly until mixture boils again. Remove from heat. Stir in butter
and vanilla.

4 Slice bananas and layer half of them on the graham-cracker crust.
Pour half the hot custard over bananas and arrange remaining bananas
over custard. Pour remaining custard over top layer of bananas.
Refrigerate overnight.

5 One hour before serving, whip heavy cream and vanilla until stiff.
Top custard with cream and refrigerate.

Yield: one 9-inch pie

Lime Pie

This pie is light and airy. It's wonderful after a heavy meal or on a hot summer night.

One 9-inch graham-cracker crust
½ cup fresh lime juice
1 package unflavored gelatin

3 eggs, separated
One 14-ounce can sweetened
   condensed milk

1 Prepare crust (see page 105) and set aside.

2 In a small saucepan heat lime juice; add gelatin to dissolve.

3 In a large bowl, beat egg yolks for 10 minutes or until light yellow and fluffy. Add gelatin mixture and sweetened condensed milk. Stir well.

4 In a separate bowl, beat egg whites until stiff. Fold them into the lime-juice mixture. Pour into prepared pie crust and refrigerate at least 1 hour. Serve plain or with whipped cream.

Yield: one 9-inch pie

Lemon Cream Pie

This pie features whipped cream, crunchy meringue,
and a tart lemon filling—the best of everything!

Meringue Crust

4 egg whites	¾ cup granulated sugar
¼ teaspoon cream of tartar	

Filling

5 egg yolks	1 tablespoon grated lemon rind
⅓ cup fresh lemon juice	1½ cups heavy cream
¼ cup granulated sugar	1 teaspoon vanilla extract
2 tablespoons butter	3 tablespoons granulated sugar

1 Preheat oven to 275° F.

2 *To prepare crust:* Beat egg whites until frothy. Add cream of tartar and beat until stiff. Add sugar and beat meringue again.

3 Butter a 9-inch pie pan and spoon meringue into pan, shaping it like a pie shell. Bring the sides up high so that it will hold all the filling. (The meringue will bake exactly as you shape it.)

4 Bake for 1 hour, or until meringue is firm and golden brown. Remove from oven and cool.

5 *To prepare filling:* In the top of a double boiler over boiling water, combine egg yolks, lemon juice, sugar, and butter. Stir constantly until thick and custardy. Stir in lemon rind.

6 In a separate bowl, beat cream until stiff, add vanilla and sugar, and beat again. Spread half the cream in the meringue shell. Spread lemon custard on cream. Pile remaining cream on top of custard and refrigerate for 24 hours before serving.

Yield: one 9-inch pie

Chocolate-Chip Pie

I made this pie before I opened my store in 1980. My Dad said it would never sell because people like fruit pies. During my first year in business this turned out to be one of our biggest sellers—because it was different. I describe it to customers as a cross between a brownie, a cookie, and fudge. It's very rich, so serve small slices.

1 unbaked 9-inch pie shell (see Pie Pastry, page 104)
2 eggs
½ cup all-purpose flour
⅓ cup granulated sugar
⅓ cup firmly packed dark-brown sugar
¾ cup butter, melted and cooled
1 cup semisweet chocolate chips
1 cup chopped walnuts

1 Preheat oven to 325° F.

2 If making shell from scratch, use one-half recipe Pie Pastry. Set shell aside.

3 In a large bowl, beat eggs. Add flour and sugars. Mix well. Add butter and stir. Stir in chocolate chips and walnuts. Pour mixture into prepared pie crust.

4 Bake for 1 hour, or until center is firm. Remove pan to wire rack to cool. Serve with vanilla or coffee ice cream, if desired.

Yield: one 9-inch pie

Chocolate Cream Pie

This is one of my Mom's favorite desserts. If the August rush isn't too crazy, I like to make this for her birthday instead of a cake. It's very fudgy, smooth, and dense.

1 prebaked 9-inch pie shell (see Pie Pastry, page 104)
1 cup granulated sugar
½ cup plus 2 tablespoons all-purpose flour
½ teaspoon salt

2½ cups milk
3 squares (3 ounces) unsweetened chocolate, chopped
3 egg yolks, beaten
1 teaspoon vanilla extract
2 tablespoons butter

Topping

1 cup heavy cream
½ teaspoon vanilla extract

1 tablespoon granulated sugar

---

1 If making shell from scratch, use one-half recipe Pie Pastry. Set shell aside.

2 Prick crust with a fork to vent. Place a piece of waxed paper on bottom and cover with uncooked rice. Bake in a preheated 400° F. oven for 20 minutes or until golden. Remove pan to a wire rack to cool.

3 In the top of a double boiler over boiling water combine sugar, flour, and salt. Mix well. Gradually stir in milk. Add chopped chocolate. Cook, stirring constantly, until mixture is smooth and thick; remove from heat.

4 Gradually stir 1 cup of hot mixture into the beaten egg yolks. Add egg mixture back to the chocolate mixture. Return to double boiler and cook until mixture begins to boil. Remove from heat and stir in vanilla and butter. Pour into prepared pie shell and refrigerate at least 3 hours.

5 One hour before serving, whip heavy cream, vanilla, and sugar until stiff. Pile cream on top of pie filling, spreading to all the edges of the pie crust. Refrigerate until ready to serve.

Yield: one 9-inch pie

Tart Lemon
Meringue Pie

This pie is only for lemon lovers. It's light, smooth, and very tart.

1 prebaked 9-inch pie shell (see
   Pie Pastry, page 104)
¾ cup granulated sugar
¼ cup cornstarch
¼ teaspoon salt
1 cup cold water
1 cup fresh lemon juice

4 egg yolks, lightly beaten
3 tablespoons butter
1 tablespoon fresh lemon rind
4 egg whites
¼ teaspoon cream of tartar
¼ cup granulated sugar

1 Preheat oven to 400° F.

2 If making shell from scratch, use one-half recipe Pie Pastry.

3 Prick crust with a fork to vent. Place a piece of waxed paper on crust and cover with rice. Bake for 20 minutes, or until golden. Remove pan to wire rack to cool. Set oven at 325° F.

4 In the top of a double boiler over boiling water combine sugar, cornstarch, and salt. Gradually add water and lemon juice. Whisk until smooth. Cook mixture, stirring constantly, until it thickens. Gradually add 1 cup hot mixture to lightly beaten egg yolks and stir. Add egg mixture back to lemon mixture in double boiler and cook until mixture just begins to boil. Remove from heat and stir in butter and lemon rind.

5 Pour hot filling into prepared pie crust. Set aside.

6 *Make meringue:* In a large bowl, beat egg whites until frothy. Add cream of tartar and gradually add sugar. Beat until peaks lean over lightly when beaters are lifted.

7 Spread meringue over hot filling, sealing it at all the edges of the pie shell. Bake for 10 minutes, or until meringue is lightly browned. Cool pie on wire rack slightly before refrigerating.

Yield: one 9-inch pie

Chocolate Mallow Pie

My brother's mother-in-law, Elva Kibbe, brings this pie every year for Thanksgiving. I have to admit that we all go for this one before taking the pies I bring from the bake shop. I think we get burned out on apple and pumpkin by the time Thanksgiving day actually arrives. For a very high pie, use the 9-inch shell.

1 prebaked 9- or 10-inch pie shell
    (see Pie Pastry, page 104)
3 squares (3 ounces) unsweetened
    chocolate
1 package plain gelatin
⅓ cup cold water

½ cup granulated sugar
⅔ cup corn syrup
1 teaspoon vanilla extract
1 cup heavy cream

Topping

1 cup heavy cream
½ teaspoon vanilla

1 tablespoon granulated sugar
    (optional)

---

1 Preheat oven to 400° F.

2 If making shell from scratch, use one-half recipe Pie Pastry.

3 Prick crust with a fork to vent. Place a piece of waxed paper on crust and cover with rice. Bake for 20 minutes, or until golden. Remove pan to wire rack to cool.

4 Melt chocolate in top of a double boiler over boiling water and cool slightly.

5 Soften gelatin in the cold water in top of a double boiler and add sugar. Heat until dissolved. Put corn syrup, vanilla, and gelatin mixture in a large bowl. Beat at high speed with an electric mixer for 10 minutes or until mixture is a soft, marshmallow consistency. Fold in melted chocolate.

6 In a separate bowl beat cream until stiff. Fold into chocolate mixture. Pour into prebaked pie shell and chill for several hours.

7 *To prepare topping:* About 1 hour before serving, beat cream, vanilla, and sugar (if desired) until stiff. Spread evenly on top of pie and refrigerate.

Yield: one 9- or 10-
inch pie

Index